T0279686

GROW UP

GROW UP

Becoming the Parent

Your Kids Deserve

GARY JOHN BISHOP

HarperOne
An Imprint of HarperCollins*Publishers*

HarperCollins books may be purchased for educational, business, or sales promotional use. For information, please email the Special Markets Department at SPsales@harpercollins.com.

FIRST EDITION

Designed by Janet Evans-Scanlon

Library of Congress Cataloging-in-Publication Data is available upon request.

ISBN 978-0-06-321556-6

23 24 25 26 27 LBC 5 4 3 2 1

This book is dedicated to those who are committed to growth, even when the world says it's not possible. Fuck them, you got this.

Contents

GROW UP

"Reality is created by the mind. We can change our reality by changing our mind."

—*Plato*

A REALITY AMONG MANY

It doesn't matter how many parenting books you've read, how many mom groups you've joined on Facebook, what your kid whisperer qualifications are, or how blue your chakra is, being a parent is the single most challenging job you'll ever take on in your life, and whatever toolbox you think you've managed to piece together, for many people there's just not enough in there to see them through it with some relative peace of mind.

Why is that?

Because whatever you have learned is intertwined with your own upbringing, which means you are either furiously trying to replicate your own childhood or trying somehow to overcome it with your kids, a mechanism that will undoubtedly need undoing if we are to make any headway here.

We will undo it by showing you it in all its glory. Why you do what you do, how you do what you do, and ultimately why all of it will make little or no difference to the outcome you are after.

In terms of a challenge, the job of being a parent is most closely followed by getting over being *raised* by parents, which points to why this book is a must for all human beings, regardless of their parental status.

Like it or not, you are shaped by the cultural ideal of what a parent should or shouldn't be, even if you have no kids of your own. This is mainly because we see them in movies or on TV; read about them in books, magazines, and newspapers; and well, aren't they just about everywhere you go? Then there's the lifetime you've spent comparing your parents to that often-damaging cultural ideal. That's why this book, while primarily for parents or people with that aim, actually applies to all people.

Trying to build a life in the aftermath of whatever job *your* parents did or didn't do with you during your formative years is pretty much the bulk of what people are dealing with, whether it seems that way or not. Much, if not all, of the personal growth work you will ever do in your life is directly or indirectly related to the experiences you had during your first twenty years or so on this planet.

Most people get stuck in the backwash of their past traumas and dogmas, beliefs and half-truths, stories, excuses, and superstitions, which then become the framework for how we raise our children. We survive, we adjust, and somehow become accustomed to the environment. We forget the magic of the new and the endless horizon of possibility that once stretched far beyond our keenest line of sight.

Whatever we are left with becomes our reality. How in the hell does one even begin to change that?

You can't change the past after all. Right?

Maybe, but if the past lives on in our mind, and as Plato points out, you can change your mind, then . . .

However, I'm not going to blow a fairy tale up your bum here. In these pages, we'll lay out all the ways you can change your mind. Some will be simple; others will be challenging and difficult and, for some, seem impossible. The real conflict will not be the words in the book but rather your willingness to absorb them and create a real mindset shift for yourself.

Changing it will ultimately be up to you, but the choice to do so will be yours and yours alone. This book will help you recover that lost ground, tainted by life. To take back the once rich and bountiful pastures of imagination and verve and purpose and put them back in front of you to explore and create your own future. And to empower you to teach your children to do the same.

> *"We are our choices."*
> *–Jean-Paul Sartre*

This Is Still a SELF-Help Book

And so . . . here we are. Another book in an ocean of books about parenting. Or not. Let me shed some light on what makes this one so strikingly different.

First, you can thank God this is not one of the chorus of others brimming with monochromatic tips on being the best mom or dad, doing this or doing that, watching out for this or that, tucking, folding, swaddling, and psycho parenting 101, 102, or 5150, washed down with a hearty mouthful of Chardonnay-flavored quotes about how they used to do it in the good old days. Bear in mind, how they did it back then was how you (and a helluva lot of other people) were raised. And look at how that special little circus of the weird has worked out, right?

See Twitter for details.

I mean not all *that* bad, but given how much of your parenting boils down to you working out ways you can convince your children to avoid making the mistakes you made or sidestepping the past you had, maybe a significant part of this parenting stuff is unpacking what's swirling around in your head about the subject?

You'd be amazed at what you've decided is true about this matter without any kind of questioning.

In the domain of human affairs, you're often unable to take a new direction until you fully comprehend what has been driving you in the old one. But it's not just driving you. This is one of those things that applies to all of us.

That's definitely true when it comes to parenting.

Breaking down the enigma of *who* is doing the job (rather than telling you *how* to do it, which is what makes most of the other parenting books completely useless) is what makes where we are starting here all the more interesting and ultimately useful. The point is, when you get to the murky bottom of *who* you are, your personal magic fun bucket, the job itself becomes a whole lot clearer and inspiring and free.

You'll also get a profound understanding of everyone who had the job before you and your responsibility to those who are to follow. Yes, it's *that* big and it's *that* important.

Let me make one thing patently clear. This book is not for you to insist your parents read or for you to give to your children in the forlorn hope that it will fix the shit you've been pointing to about them. This book is completely, entirely, and 100 percent for you to see where you are in this equation and to make a fucking change not only as a parent but also as a decent, grounded human being.

That's it.

You change and everything else changes.

There will be times when you're digesting the implications of what I'm proposing, when you start to panic about what you should do with your kids to free them from what we uncover about yourself here.

Let go of that anxiety long enough to get to the end of the book. All will be revealed.

Here we'll take on this whole notion of the *being* of a parent—that is, the kind of human being you'll have to be to get this done. We'll work on unearthing all of the mental blocks, old emotions, and superstitious nonsense that get in the way of it.

And do a whole lot of letting go.

What You Need to Know

We're tackling the subject of "parent" (as opposed to an A–Z guide for parenting) both for the parents (and stepparents) among you to finally become the kind of presence you need to be, and for everyone else to get a complete sense of the "why" of your parents beyond the tired and drama-rich story many people put together over the years. Those of you who manage to do the double here get twice the results for the same price.

What a deal, huh?

This not a "how to" book but rather a "WTF" edition. I don't do "how-to" because in many ways, what you are experiencing as a parent (or/and the child of one) is a function of what you have put together in your own head, built upon a mostly invisible story line manifesting in your life as thoughts, feelings, and habits that you just seem to automatically respond to whenever they come up.

And boy, do they come up!

You are not a direct product of your past. And while it is true you were born (thrown) into an already existing conversation of family and values and morality and so on, you are in fact a predictable, repetitive emotional expression of what you have come to *believe* as true about all of that past. And no, what you have come to believe about back then is not the same as what actually happened.

You should read what I just said a thousand times. Then again. And again. Then think. Then read it again.

Therefore, what you now *believe* about your childhood is your biggest problem. What happened is just what happened. Them's the facts. What people believe about all of that is where they begin to disconnect. Your "story" of the past often produces overwhelming fear, confusion, anxiety, frustration, anger and a host of other negative patterns that fool you into thinking you urgently need to solve the symptoms when in fact you never really get to the heart of the matter. The story. Not the past.

And if you are striving to become a fundamentally better parent, you need to realize you are in a tired matrix that really needs to fucking go. But it won't go without a fight, and be left in no doubt, you'll fight for that shitrix without even realizing that's what you're up to.

That's when you need to wake up.

To give you some context, let me warn you in advance.

I'll be getting into some very touchy stuff for some of you in these pages. A few of you precious souls have already been hooked. Oh, well. If you know anything about my work, you know I'm willing to get into the dirt with you and slug it out. No fake platitudes or meaningless phrases that do little more than tickle your molecules.

We're exorcising ghosts and building futures.

We'll start by uncovering the story we've told ourselves: understanding our propensity to blame, understanding where our parents came from, understanding that our version of our childhood is imbued with weight by ourselves, *not* the events, and finally, doing the work with forgiving the past and our parents.

Then we need to understand how we got our story as we tell it today. We'll do this by exploring the three waves of childhood and how each shape us into the people we are today. I'll leave you with a better way to be a parent: by doing it from a state of being that includes love, forgiveness, and integrity.

And finally, we see what it looks like to be an authentic parent, full stop.

What's the job of being a parent? That your kids come out of this robust and equipped. While they, like all people, will have their scars and bumps (as they're supposed to), they are grounded in who they authentically are and why they are because they witnessed you handle it too.

"Children begin by loving their parents; as they grow older, they judge them; sometimes they forgive them."

—Oscar Wilde

"Small-minded people habitually reproach others for their own misfortunes. Average people reproach themselves. Those that are dedicated to a life of wisdom understand that the impulse to blame something or someone is foolishness, that there is nothing to be gained in blaming, whether it be others or oneself."

—Epictetus

FROM THE ASHES OF BLAME

We have to start by uncovering what the story is we've been telling ourselves about our childhood, our parents, and how we were raised. The main problem with this notion is that we think it's mostly other people who are living their story.

For us, we don't have a story. We have the facts. Right?

No.

Think about that as it applies to your own life. It can start with something as simple as describing your childhood in general terms. Would you say you had a good childhood, or a bad one?

Let's say you had a "good" one. That's an opinion. A view that describes a series of events. Whatever the view, that's where you get located. Mentally, you are in bed with your own view.

Most would never challenge that particular view because it appears positive, but it's as much a narrative as any others. If you dig a little deeper, were your parents loving and kind? Harsh and cruel? Or somewhere in the middle? Again, this is all narrative, put together to capture years of a childhood. No matter what you arrived at, how did that story shape you?

It gets worse. How is it still shaping you?

Notice the attention we're giving the story here. As you'll find in the coming chapters, the language you automatically use to describe any area of life is fully reflected in your emotional state. So you speak, so you be. Everyone wants to change but can't quite get their head around changing their attachment to their story. Why? Because they're trying to change emotions or behaviors. Wrong end of the stick.

Who have you become in your story?

Whatever your answers are here, these are the foundation stones of your story.

And if you lay this out in front of yourself, you'll start to see that there's someone or something you still blame for the parts of your childhood that weren't exactly perfect.

Blame is a funny thing.

Not in a comedic, ha-ha kind of way but rather in a quirky, dark, nefarious sense. We know we shouldn't blame. An old friend of mine once said something while we were both working through "stuff" from our burdensome pasts. "I don't blame my dad for how my life turned out but it's definitely his fault."

We laugh about that to this day.

Blame can be obvious and fiery and abrasive. It can also be subtle and nuanced and in many ways a comfort. We can speak in terms of blame, and it sounds just like we're sharing "how it was," but it doesn't take much to connect where the finger is pointing.

I've coached many people through this distinction who started with "I don't blame anyone at all for my life because I had a happy childhood," all of which is a narrative as much as any other. No matter your past, someone, somewhere is on the hook for it and it really is on you to uncover what all of that is and how it plays out in your life. If you've read any of my other books, some of this will sound familiar, because blame touches every area of your life, and releasing yourself from blame is so critical to moving forward. So don't blow past this.

Of course, the next part of that is taking ownership for that life of finger pointing and to finally embrace all of it as yours. But let's not get too far ahead of ourselves here.

Blame really is a critical component of the dark arts for being a human being in a world where being blameless equals being free from judgment and scrutiny. Safety in innocence.

You see, we are tribal. We gravitate to groups we identify with and yes, loners are only ever loners against the dynamic of the group. If there's no tribe then there's no such thing as a loner. The very idea of tribe is what gives us the notion of the independent being. It all starts in group.

I read a particularly fascinating article on human development that found evidence of Neanderthals gathering in very small groups to exist, something between 10 and 30 individuals. The theory is that they were stronger and faster than their Homo sapien neighbors and so were individually better equipped to handle the ever-threatening wilds of the world at that time.

Homo sapiens, on the other hand, gathered in groups in excess of 120. Why? The simple answer seems to be that belonging to a bigger group meant a better chance at survival given their very obvious physical disadvantages.

That larger, more complex community is also believed to be the reason why Homo sapiens developed a much more sophisticated ability to converse and, as we'll get into later, language is the place where human beings can distinguish one thing from another. Everything has a name and a meaning, and our growth as a species is very much about giving new language to things that, for us, never existed in our vocabulary. As we articulate, we capture new realms of imagination and investigation and with them new growth as a species.

I digress.

To be included is to be safe and to be excluded means to be at risk. Exclusion for us is connected to threat, which is why we often struggle to reconcile rejection in all its forms.

All too often it *feels* like we're going to die when we are rejected.

On the other hand, when we blame, we experience a certain safety, which cannot be ignored. It's closely tied to *being right* in that regard. The secret sauce to survival for a human being is to stay clear of blame and judgment. And how I might do that is simply by convincing *you* that it's not my fault, to have the consensus agree with my innocence such that I remain in the group. Free from judgment and threat.

Even at another's expense.

If the group (or authority) does not agree, I may be rejected and expelled from the group into what feels like a very real danger to life itself. That's why breakups, being the odd one out, going through middle school, starting a new job, being fired from an old job and any one of a litany of social situations can poke and prod at our primordial desire for survival and not being singled out or left behind.

There's a straight line from judgment, blame, and social exclusion all the way to crime, punishment, and imprisonment. Same shit, really.

Being excluded from society, from the safety of the group is supposed to be the deterrent. That's how powerful it really is. Unfortunately, those we seclude in society just join another tribe.

We punish in our everyday lives by excluding too. Those little moments when you storm off or don't answer the phone or texts, when you "teach them a lesson" in one way or another are all designed to take away power, to get leverage, and to leave the target with the experience of being judged, wrong, excluded, and . . . ultimately threatened. Ugh.

Your silent treatment? Yep, same effect.

And this stuff is with the people we supposedly love! Fuck me.

If you're using seclusion, isolation, or whatever else you want to call it, as a way to teach your kids consequences for their actions, you may want to give that shit a rethink. In fact, if you're turning to that as a strategy for anyone . . . I think it's fair to say a lesson in communication and authenticity could go a long way and give you some real power to deal with situations where you don't have much.

Into the Dark

But there's another side to blame that very few ever consider, and it's a doozy.

Blame is the catalyst for keeping you tied to what has been.

To blame is to perpetuate the past, to keep it going. And you're a fucking blame machine. Join the dots.

> *"All this hurrying from place to place won't bring you any relief, for you're traveling in the company of your own emotions, followed by your troubles all the way."*
> *—Seneca*

That past could be ten minutes ago or thirty years ago. We blame in an instant and can keep it going during a lifetime. Sometimes we become so used to it, so entrenched in its toxic allure, it doesn't even feel like we're blaming anymore. But we are.

Blame is an emotional signpost. A place of reference we become attached to. The first chapter in an unfolding story that can go on and on and on, often at a terrible cost. It clings to you like a fucking alien on your face and cries loudly for its own importance.

"But it WAS their fault."

"They ARE in the wrong."

"I'll NEVER forgive them!"

And on and on and on it goes, spinning away in your head, fucking with your heart, and keeping you stuck. One of the reasons why many people cannot let go of the blame lifestyle is because they cannot see the true extent of the damage they are doing to themselves.

It seems like you're getting out of this intact while they are getting the pain. It's in fact the opposite.

But it's not just blaming people. We blame situations and circumstances too.

"I'm not good with money, I grew up poor."

"I was the youngest in my family, so . . ."

"I was the oldest in my family, so . . ."

Again, doesn't seem like blame, does it? I mean, it just seems like we're telling it like it is, but we're not. The branches of emotion that sprawl out and into our lives to caress, explain, and justify everything we do or don't do.

All the while ensuring we escape the scrutiny of being judged and the subterranean threat of being singled out and in the spotlight of other people's opinions. It completely gets us off the hook for who we are now, for the life we have and opportunities we missed.

The kind of person you are and the life you have come equipped with explanation. And blame.

Sometimes we explain ourselves in terms of a person and what they did or did not do (often this is a parent or a parent figure), a situation, and all that it did or did not do to you, or even in terms of society or the world itself. And it's a stimulating line of reasoning, one that you will find plenty of allies for.

Keep in mind that we are shining a light on the kind of thing most people just shrug and learn to live with, but we won't do that here. Some of the most important work any human being can do for themselves will require not only introspection but also the courage to be with the uncomfortable truths that percolate beneath the surface of all of our excuses, reasons, and justifications.

Now, on one hand, blame is a logical place for people to land, which is why so many see the rationale in assigning criticism for your past to a certain individual or circumstance, which all too fluidly will then lead you down the long and laborious pathway of work to recover or to heal.

Authentic Healing

Of course, there are lots of ways by which one can heal, but we'll go with the everyday, most common version that most people engage with.

In this model, recovery is always from the perspective of seeing yourself in the role of the recovering victim or the repentant sinner. You'll *always* have to be one or the other. Think about that. Is it any wonder why we're all seeking nourishment from the mass trough of "healing" and "recovery" and "positivity" and "hope"?

And those have been your only real choices. Get over "it" and/or somehow get over yourself. Ugh.

We're not doing any of that. We're deconstructing blame. Dissolving and disappearing the construct so we can get right into the juice of self-realization and truth and personal power. To get you grounded in your own expression of what it is to be a parent. And a functioning person.

If you cannot wean yourself off the artificial high of "blame," this is not the book you thought it would be, but it is still the one for you. Maybe you should start embracing the idea of finally shifting yourself off that hill you've been dying on for so long.

Living your life through gritted teeth is no way to live.

Why is it so critically important for you to take stock of this blame thing? For some of you, releasing the *need* for blame will result in an instant transformation. Instant freedom from the past simply because if there's no blame, there's nothing to get yourself wrapped up in. You're free, you're done, and everyone can get on with their lives. Some others will have to work through this a bit because they either insist that there *should* be blame (and are therefore willfully tying themselves to the bullshit) or they haven't dug deeply enough to see who or what they are still blaming.

If you're currently squirreling yourself away in the safe ambiguity of those who feel that they "can't," replace "can't" with "won't" and you'll see you're on the side of "willfully tying" no matter how much you may try to squirm away from its icy glare.

You see, you were born into a culture of blame, which gives rise to the twin cities of shame and guilt. Therefore I'm obviously not even blaming you here. As human beings, these are very much our go-to survival outlets. That you feel these things is predictable, sometimes debilitating, but ultimately boring as fuck. There's nothing remarkable about shame, nothing extraordinary about guilt, and absolutely zero personal power in blame.

Blame is the crack of human emotional states. It doesn't matter who or what you are blaming, even yourself.

All you need is just a casual, solitary hit, then another, then another, and before you know it, you get lost in that shit. Then you and your friends and confidantes can huddle together in your fake comforting little blame crack house and throw whoever and whatever you need to under the bus just so you can temporarily shelter yourself from the crushing and relentless press of ownership for your current state. Yet you cannot hide from it.

Is it a bit extreme to compare something like blame to drug addiction? No. It's fucking not.

Can you even begin to imagine the families that have been destroyed by this phenomenon? The businesses that have crashed, careers lost, the broken health and well-being of countless people scattered across the planet, let alone the violence, manipulation, and yes, even wars that have been marked throughout history in the myopic pursuit of who is to blame. Fuck the carnage, huh?

The disconnect from the damage of blame in people's lives is more like a chasm than a fracture. And the resulting devastation is dulled by explanation, justification, and poor logic while simultaneously being staunchly defended to the death by those who agree with the pursuit or those who are numbed by confusion and deadness and suffering.

Are you getting this? I know, we're barely a few fucking pages in, and shit's getting real, right? This is serious because your life is serious business. It's all on the line right now and I need you here for all of it.

People *say* they want to change, people *say* they need things to be different, but when they begin to confront what that will actually take, all too often they meekly sink back down into the deep, dark lake of despair and apathy. Don't be people. Be brave, think, and come to the freaking light.

Set a life marker here. A point of no return, a bold commitment to the new and empowering.

Let this sink in:

Finding someone to blame for the situation you were born into or were even raised in is bankrupt. It just isn't workable for you to blame this life on that one, and at some level you already know this. Drawing a straight line between the pain of then and the life you have now is over. It has to be or the life you have will always be tainted by the one you believe you had no matter how many mantras you chant.

Read that as many times as you need to.

We often feel that if we let go of our desire to blame, we are somehow making what happened okay. It's like your parent handed you a burning coal and you're hanging onto it so they can see how much they burned you. And it still burns. And you're still holding on.

And you're waiting for an apology or to be heard or to be acknowledged or seen or understood. And it burns. And you're holding on. And then someone like me comes along and tells you about blame, and you feel the pain and you see the logic, but you begin arguing for your pain. And you're burning. And on this bullshit goes.

It's not hard to connect the dots here to see why we can't quite hit the mark as the parents we would like to be.

If you were free from your past, what kind of parent could you be? If you were free from the past, what kind of parent would you have? It's all tied together by blame. Freedom lies on the other side of all of it.

If this is pissing you off, good. Wake the hell up. Where do you think that stuff has been stewing? Oh, you think you're good and that this stuff only really bothers you from time to time when it comes up? Dude, someone shit in the electric cooking pot of your life, and all the positive gravy in the world will not hide it. Get a handle on yourself.

Still can't let it go? Welcome to the hamster wheel. You're the one who will ultimately pay.

I'm not saying this like some kind of threat. It's a cold reality for people that, if you fail to face, will ultimately hurt you. That's the trade that's constantly on the table.

You'll cash in your potential, your vigor, your sense of hope and peace of mind, and you'll regularly convince yourself you are "fine" and that it's worth it and that you are right, but in reality you've numbed yourself to how you're living and what it's costing you.

People are generally looking for life change ideas they can just "plug in" and play, but that approach is just jaded and weak. You need to dive into the mess, rake through the slurry of drama and ugliness and fucking deal with yourself.

That baggage is real, and it has an impact. If you are already feeling guilt or shame or anger or hopelessness, gird your fucking loins because we're going into the breach.

By way of support, I want you to know it can be different for you, but let me start with this. If you can let go of that base desire to blame and demonstrate that way of living in a real and palpable way, you may well be teaching your own kids the most valuable lesson they will ever learn. That their authentic happiness is their own. How can you pass on some sense of happiness if you're not happy? Same with forgiveness and compassion and connection. I know you think you are teaching them one thing when in reality you're passing along tips on how they should treat you when the shit hits the fan.

And it likely will.

I'll get into this notion of breaking a generational chain later, but getting your ass off the blame trail is key to everything.

Freedom begins with giving up the idea of who is to blame. Right now.

"Small-minded people blame others, average people blame themselves, the wise see all blame as foolishness."

—Epictetus

THE PROBLEM WITH PARENTS

No one sets out to fuck their children up. *And* sometimes that's what happens.

People get lost in the fog of their own lives, strained and pained and pressed, just like you have done at times.

Sometimes they end up dominated by their own demons to the degree of impacting their own peace of mind and grounded logic. They often become the kind of adult they had no intention of ever becoming when their life started. I'm not justifying or excusing anyone here. Shit happens, and as we've already discussed, how many people are truly equipped for the life they ended up with? Are you?

I am also completely clear that while there are those who have acted in ways that are thoroughly irresponsible, selfish, harsh, and at times even illegal, the reality is that all people, just like you, are forging a life to free themselves of the shackles of what has been. That they end up completely out of tune with how their kids are developing is not only predictable but also in line with a tired and jaded logic that is in dire need of a transformation.

Then there are the people whose mental health, for whatever reason, is trailing hopelessly behind the job at hand and just do not function with a capacity for what is in front of them. The cold reality is in the numbers. One in twenty-five Americans lives with what could be described as a "serious mental illness," while one in five Americans is likely to deal with some sort of mental health issue in their lifetime.

Whether you or your parents dealt with such a thing, whether your situation was mild or catastrophic, the desire to turn to the dynamic of the recovering victim or repentant sinner has to be resisted. No matter who is who in your story and no matter how appealing that dynamic may be for you.

Now, of course, I'm out to cast a wide net so as many people as possible can hear themselves in this conversation, but I really don't need to because this applies to all people anyway, regardless of their situation. This is also not designed to let you off the hook for your life or someone else off the hook for theirs. That's the blame train and we're off that loco motion, remember?

I'm not doing radical forgiveness either. While that's a powerful option, you'll see in the coming chapters why it is completely unnecessary here. Some of you are so dug in with your drama, I can hear the sigh of relief from an ocean away. Something there for you to learn too, I might add.

You just don't get to let go of the constraints of the past and hold onto them at the same time.

Like you, all parents have a past. Also like you, the vast majority of those people are both incomplete with that past and fundamentally unclear as to how it is playing out in their life. Sure, some may *know* this but like most of the stuff that people know, very little of that knowledge is actually making a difference or acting as inspiration for real change. People just go around in life making the best of what they got stuck with (aka pretending without ever realizing it's really all a pretense) or partially awake but caught in the cycle of suffering and fixing, suffering and fixing, on and on and on.

One of the challenging things with reconciling the job your parents did or did not do is that it is seen through a child's eyes. All too often people spend their lifetime engaging with their parents through those same eyes, no matter how mature or philosophical they become.

It's little wonder the past lives on.

So let's look at your situation.

It's in the Numbers

Before 1990 the average age for a parent was under twenty-five years of age. Some were considerably younger, some older, but if most of those folks were about twenty-three or twenty-four, a pretty decent case can be made that the vast majority of people were still trying to work themselves out when they became a parent. Again, no excuses, just what's so. Look at any young person in the twenty-to-twenty-five age range.

That's pretty much how your parents looked when you arrived.

If you were born in 1990 or before, the average age for a parent gets younger and younger with every couple of decades or so.

"So what, Mr. Scottish person?"

I'll tell you what. Google the average twenty-three, twenty-four, or twenty-five-year-old human being. Look at some decidedly stereotypical images. What do you see?

I already did. Here's what it looks like: youth; naïveté; hope.

Young people beginning their big adult adventure. What you cannot see is their baggage, their trauma, their already built-in shame or anger or determination to prove something or someone wrong. Add their fears and misgivings and a smattering of being bullied, abused, or assaulted, and hey presto! Ready for life.

And then you show up.

But you didn't see youth or vitality or the lingering echoes of innocence in their faces. You couldn't see their trauma or baggage. To you this was just Mom and Dad.

My parents were like every other human being on the face of the planet. Living the life that was right in front of their faces, encumbered by their own past, trying somehow to make it. They had their own burdens, and in the melee of life it's all too easy for our children to become another of those weights they must bear. Could I see any of that as a kid? No, but I could let my mind begin to understand as a fully fledged adult now, couldn't I? I started to wonder what life was like for my dad. Both of his parents were deaf, and he was taken away from them when he was young. He was a kid growing up in the United Kingdom during the Second World War, which was a time of a very real existential threat to that nation. The government decided to protect the children in the most obvious but dramatic way. The plan was to physically remove them as targets. It was called Operation Pied Piper and entailed evacuating tens of thousands of children from locations deemed at risk from military attack across the country and sending them to foster homes in rural parts of the country. Or abroad.

Some of those kids went to places such as Canada or Australia or the United States.

Some never returned.

My dad went to the highlands of Scotland to live on a farm, and while on one hand that may be considered as idyllic, there was a whole other side of that to consider.

You see, the parents did not accompany their children. They were separated.

I started to imagine that nine-year-old boy being put on a train not knowing if he would return weeks, months, or years later, or if he would ever see his parents alive again. Fuck me. What was that like for him, his parents, his older brothers, who all stayed behind? How did all of that land in his little head? What was his first night in that foster home like? I'll never truly know. But I do know he had many internal struggles throughout his adult life, and I often wondered if he was left stuck with something from that time that he could never quite shake off.

Imagine this happening to your children right now. Let that sink in. How do you think your little ones would react to being split from you? What would your first night without them at home be like?

The potential for this to be traumatic is not hard to imagine. Some kids deal with this nightmare even now. Separated, alone and afraid.

For my mom, she had to deal with the impact of the death of her own mother when she was only two or three years old. Never knowing the loving arms of her real mom. What was she left with? How did that impact her? Her father remarried, she became part of a combined family. And remember, this was at a time when people were just expected to "get on with it," no fucking therapy sessions or methodology for calming a frayed baby heart.

Her life was a never-ending experience of feeling unloved, and no matter how many times she may have heard the opposite, it just never got in. A prisoner to her own past.

Life back then was harsh and unforgiving, and both these little ones somehow had to just deal with it. Then they grew up. And they became my parents.

You, like most people who grew up with their parents as the fount of all knowledge, the all-seeing, all-knowing center of the universe where everything is fair, balanced, and a shining example of the wisdom of the ages. Like a cool Moses or queen of Sheba.

At least initially.

Then it changed. In a moment of time. At some point in your early life, you witnessed some perceived "flaw" in them. It stuck. Then you questioned who they were, and the tumble of opinions began, and with them a lifetime of unconsciously gathering evidence in their favor. They flowed seamlessly into your mind and became the truth for you. And they're still there, anchored in your thoughts and shaping all that you have become to this day.

For me, it was an argument I witnessed my parents having when I was young that kicked everything off. I'll go more into that in chapter 5.

Now, I'm not saying your parents didn't contribute to what you were seeing and hearing but you, like all human beings, once you are locked into a certain flaw you see in another, you struggle to see or hear anything that goes against that or that could, God forbid, bankrupt your observation.

Once you form that view, you're a little truffle pig for more of the same. Blinkers on, snout down, and off you go. Oink, oink.

You did what everyone did and is likely to do in the future. Yes, your kids too.

You could have been four or ten or seventeen when this happened. It doesn't matter, and if your parents are like most people, they either barely noticed your new eyes or found themselves arguing against them.

There's invariably a point in this conversation where readers take sides: their own.

They begin to interact with what I'm saying from a position, the same one they have stood in for most of their life. Now, like a lot of what I point to, most of what you deal with in life is from the human perspective rather than a personal one. You're not the way you are because of the life you've had; you are the way you are because that's the natural order of things for all human beings.

As I said earlier, you live your adult life either as a reflection of your childhood or in reaction to it. It's a pendulum swing of same-opposite-same-opposite-same-opposite. You're either trying to replicate what was or somehow overcome it by doing the opposite. And when something new comes along, like a new way of looking at something or a fresh understanding offering you a pathway to a completely new place for you to stand in life, it's most often received as a real threat.

Why?

Well, it's not because of your past per se but rather because of all the work you've put into building the life you have using that past as your foundation.

You are surrounded by a lot of agreement for the you you've become. People know you as you, with your opinions, traits, and beliefs, including the truth you have conditioned them to believe about you whether they were part of that past or not.

I mean if you've convinced your spouse or friends that your mom or dad was uncaring or unloving or self-absorbed or too this or too that, and now you're suddenly seeing a fresh perspective on all of that . . . you may have some undoing to do. And some of that may be particularly tricky because they've become as steeped in it as you have.

And this is common because we don't think our narrative is a narrative. We think it's a solid and undeniable re-creation of what once was. So we speak it, and every time we do, it becomes more solid and more truthful until it's just gospel.

That's how it was and that's that.

Which is why you need to take your time. And think.

"Yeah, Gary, this is all good, but when are we getting to how I can do a better job with my kids?"

If you can read between the lines here, we are already doing that. If you can't see it yet, that's okay, but try on the idea you think what you really need are some insights or "life hacks" or other such throwaway bullshit, when in reality the first (and most important) issue here is about you and freeing yourself of something. Release yourself from an all-consuming haze of old patterns that are clogging up every element of your thinking and sense of direction.

Then perhaps you could raise other human beings with the same ability. Just in case, y'know, you've fucked up a thing or two with them also.

"What upsets people is not things themselves, but their judgments about these things."

—*Epictetus*

"I have realized that the past and future are real illusions, that they exist in the present, which is what there is and all there is."

—Alan Watts

FORGIVING AN ILLUSION

This quote is one that's as close to a universal truth as I've seen anywhere. A take-it-to-the-bank kind of truth and one with which I could just end this book right here. Freedom to be yourself, freedom to be who you say you are, the kind of parent you want to be, the kind of human being you are committed to, will require you finally to deal with what is behind you because, as the Watts quote says, the intangible fog of the past is never quite behind you. It keeps showing up in the present, and while it's all a freaking illusion, it certainly doesn't feel that way at times, hence Watts's choice of words.

A real illusion. But just because the past is an illusion doesn't mean it's not real to you. What happened with your mom, or your dad, or some other pivotable figure or event has become very real and impactful to you. We need to forgive the illusion. What makes this so challenging and maybe even upsetting is how real everything about our own childhoods were.

I once made a statement that could easily be taken as hurtful or offensive or callous. It went kinda like this:

"You'll never get over your past until you confront how you use it to justify yourself."

Most people who were hooked by this could not get past how it made them feel and therefore could not dive into the rich seam of enlightenment in the spaces between these words. What's the enlightenment? The two words to focus on are "justify" and "yourself."

Every day of your life you find evidence for, and then confirm in your crevices of your mind, "you." You talk like you, walk like you, think like you, and react like . . . you. Every single day you are justifying you, and one of the main ways you do that is by reaching back into your memories to satiate that beast. Therefore the past isn't just the past. It's evidence for you being the character you have become.

It's little wonder we struggle with the idea of releasing or reframing the past because it threatens the very fabric of who you have become and exposes you to nothingness. A far too vast and uncertain space for anyone to find firm footing with. Right?

Maybe. But I digress.

So how do you, as a regular everyday human being, deal with reconciling the past?

All of the "let it go," "get over it," "prove them wrong," and whatever other stereotypical banality you may insert here, in the world doesn't quite get you to the finish line, does it? No, because the past remains as stuck and immovable as it has always been, and all the determination in the world won't change that.

It would certainly help if you could understand which specific parts of your past are having the most significant weight in your mind. For some of you, that appears easy. It would seem obvious if you've had some kind of trauma in your childhood, that it would not only be weighing heavy on you, but also be shaping all the ways you live your life, particularly your own parenting. If that's the case for you, haven't you noticed something about that stuff? Haven't you noticed that the anxiety, anger, suppression, or whatever emotional toll has become more pointed as you've gotten older? Hmmm.

Even without the obvious trauma, you can be as stuck as anyone. The machinations of a human being are the same regardless of the story line.

And when you hit that "stuckness," it is impacting whichever moment of time you are in and therefore, by default, starts to shape your idea of the future. And that's the cycle right there. The weight of the past and anxiety for the future all playing out in the present, influencing not only how you feel but also your logic, which is where you turn to for what you should and shouldn't do next. No wonder people are desperately hacking at life with all they can muster in some vain attempt at having it go their way. Confusion reigns. Desperation can set in. The past wins one way or the other.

What's the alternative?

Any Old Truth Will Do

For what it's worth I completely question the legitimacy that what you have been telling yourself is "true" about your past. I question your "truth."

That's because anyone's truth is malleable, even yours. If they can change, so can you. It's a choice. And if you keep yours, be fully aware of all that you're keeping. Pain included.

I do not question in the slightest the legitimacy of how you *feel*. Not even a smidgen. That shit's as real as real can be, and in the logic of your mind is not only well founded but also makes complete sense. Your truth and how you feel about that truth are inseparable, tied together by an unbreakable bond, and all the self-help in the world will not ease the grip of that union. They really are the toxic twins of your subconscious. There's no reconciling that past, there's no feeling better about it or any philosophy to apply that will act like a soothing balm to its permanent state of aggravation. It comes and goes, rises and dissipates. A lifetime of yoyo-ing back and forth.

You're either the sinner or the victim, remember? Sometimes both.

You just cannot keep that truth of yours and release yourself of the emotional burden of it no matter what you've been told or led to believe. If you want to feel different, you have to think different, and if you think different, you can change your mind. Rewire it even.

I can appreciate that what I'm saying here may go in the exact opposite direction of what you've read, heard, or witnessed elsewhere, but there's a reason why people use those monochromatic bumper sticker statements about moving on or forgiving or cutting out toxic people. In my not inconsiderable experience, it's all fucking bullshit. We're so easily seduced by the idea of trying to change how we feel about the past because it seems like the most logical route to freedom from it. So we listen intently for all the tips, tricks, salt baths. and latest mind tricks until there's no option but just to try to "forget" or somehow deal with the impact using positivity or gratitude or whatever else you can pull out of the old magician's hat to keep your shit together daily.

Stroke those magic fucking crystals baby.

Getting the Question Right

But what if you were to question the past itself?

That's where it gets sticky. People get dug in about what has been. They get indignant and self-righteous and pissy, sometimes caught in a helpless victimy sludge of finger-pointing and blame, and they've been doing it for so long it's all just automatic. And they do all of that even when they're trying to free themselves from it! Trapped by anger and resentment and frustration. How in the fuck are you supposed to unleash authentic love, joy, and full self-expression when you're twisted by all that you're holding onto?

Many people in this life are scouring bookstores and their ever-burgeoning Audible account for the kind of knowledge they think they need to overcome a past they have settled on without ever questioning how they got that past itself. I mean, how did you come to believe what you've come to believe as "true"?

I'll let you in on something. We don't deal in facts. We only ever deal in our *view* of facts until the *view* and the facts become one. That intertwined and coordinated explanation is what you end up being stuck with.

Let me lay this out like a giant concept and then we'll wrap it back to your real life. We need to dig through several layers here, so stay with me.

If you were to ask someone about their entire past, how long do you think it would take them to describe it to you? Ten minutes? Half an hour? Two hours? A day? A week?

Even if it were a week of nonstop talking, you and I both know you would not be getting a moment-by-moment description of events from their earliest memory all the way until the present with every conversation, flash point, and detail fully documented so you could get the whole picture.

Oh hell no, Virginia. So what would you get?

You'd get the edit. And I don't mean edited to make it easy to explain to someone. I mean the memories themselves are so heavily edited and redacted and then sequenced in the story that connect them to other parts of the edit until they all combine and compress and contort to become the story of . . . you.

And that's where most personal development work stops. Reinvent your story, reinvent yourself. While that statement may be somewhat accurate, it sometimes lands for people as dismissive or insensitive and, if you think about it, that makes sense too.

But that's just the start here, Ms. Woolf. We're just getting this thing rolling!

What gets retained? What makes it into the movie, and what gets left on the cutting room floor?

"That's easy, Gary. It's the things that traumatized or hurt or pained me the most. Those are the milestones in my memory."

Sure, that's trueish. Of course, you have lots of mundane and happy stuff in there too, but I think it's fair to say we are much more troubled by those blazing arguments, violence, abuse (of all kinds), upsets, invasions to your peace and sense of safety, of chaos and incidents of judgment than we are of that nice Christmas dinner you had when you were eight that sticks in your memory.

How the fuck does someone reinvent that "story"? Insulted yet? Hang in there. There's more.

What separates painful/not painful, traumatic/not traumatic, significant/insignificant? What makes an event or a memory unforgettable?

Think about it this way. Someone may have had an incident just like yours in their life that never quite burned its way into their mind as it did with you. And vice versa, of course. Read that again. I need you to stop right now and I need you to think. Engage here.

How could someone have an incident just like you had, yet their mind is not occupied by that in the way it does yours and in fact they might be struggling with something else entirely, something that seems way less than what you are dealing with? How can that be? Again, logic alone tells you we are not affected equally by everything that happens to us. No matter what you think of what I am saying thus far, that statement is the ground floor, where you can start to let in what I am saying.

Clearly there's something else at play in each of our editing processes. There is some element that is adding just the right amount of significance for those moments to become embedded. Whatever makes the cut has to have some weight to it, an emotional significance, but where does the weight come from?

In a moment, something happens, click, and it's in. It makes the cut.

Then another, then another, then another, and the movie starts to come together. Your adult life is about overcoming your own movie over and over. You have become so fascinated by it, so shaped and attached to the feeling of it, there's no distinction between "you" and your past anymore. They're the same thing.

What is it that's determining what is in and what is out? Psychology says "trauma," neuroscience can specify various parts of the brain associated with episodic memory and emotional locus and so on, but still I'm left with that burning question raging its way across the old frontal lobe. Of course, I'm neither a psychologist nor a neuroscientist. but neither of those explanations satisfied my thirst for something a bit more meaningful, more tangible, and usable.

The scorching questions remained: Why? Why this thing and not that thing? What distinguishes my personal experience of something from the ordinary, maybe challenging or confronting all the way through to traumatic or damaging?

What is elevating or minimizing those experiences? Simply put, you are. It's you. If you're hooked by that, go back and read the blame section again.

You unknowingly and instantly add weight in certain moments of crisis. You did it then and you still do it now. And your children are doing it as well.

What do I mean by "weight"? Basically, it adds up to a certain significance these events have for you. But what?

Many years ago, while deep in a coaching workshop, I was working with a participant. They felt they had been traumatized by their parents' divorce to such an extent that they never wanted to expose themselves to that kind of upset ever again. So they remained single, yet unhappy (yes, I'm well aware that people can be single and happy; stay with me here).

Later that same day, another participant, not related to the first, sought coaching for how to deal with their parents staying *together* when (in their view) they should have split and gotten on with their lives. That person too had remained single. And unhappy.

How do two entirely opposing circumstances produce much the same result?

When you look at the logic of how we explain how we've turned out, often the simplest of investigations will show it to be without merit, and this one is no different: We basically explain ourselves in terms of causality.

That you're this way *because* of this thing or that way *because* of that thing. But the above example blows this lazy causality out of the water. If parents divorcing was the cause of someone fearing relationships, then surely parents staying together would produce the opposite result?

"It's not any of that, Gary; it's the fucking TRAUMA!"

Scrape a bit deeper into that brain of yours, my friend, because the same thing holds true. We don't all emerge from traumatic situations with the same bruises and scars either.

So then what distinguishes one from the other?

In very simple terms, what you made it mean. That's right, YOU.

In the preceding two examples we had two very different circumstances, but each participant had concluded the same meaning. And built their life upon it.

In one case their parents had divorced. The meaning they added? Relationships are bullshit.

In the other case their parents had stayed together. The meaning they added? Relationships are bullshit.

So when did they add the meaning? Same as you. In an instant. And while they had no realization that they were doing such a thing, they did, as do you and your children. And all too often, in those traumatic moments, you are left carrying the burden of what you made it *mean*.

What did you make your own childhood mean?

About love? About trust? About yourself, or your parents?

About you?

Here's the dealio . . . you are living the life of the unconscious meaning you added, and it's so penetrative, so all-consuming, you can't see it but boy oh boy do you *feel* it!

You live a life of unconscious meaning, i.e., you are (and have been) constantly adding meaning into everything you do, see, and interact with, and mostly that meaning swings you from one predictable extreme to the next.

You got dumped on your twenty-first birthday. What did you make it mean?

Your dad took drugs. What did you make it mean about him? What about you?

When your mom calls you six times a day (or not) . . . "she's controlling" or "she doesn't really care" or "this is all for her, not for me" or . . . add your own fucking meaning; you do anyway. And you have to live with it too. The reality is that she calls you (or not). It doesn't fundamentally mean *anything*. And then you step in.

If you got fired or made fun of or you failed at this thing or that, on and on and on, one meaning piled on top of another, decades of *seemingly* navigating a life when you are in fact trying to overcome, struggle, and come to terms with what you have made it all mean in the automatic, trigger-happy depths of the subconscious.

All of which leaves you in a predictable spot that all too often includes regular burnout, isolation, resentment, overwhelm, confusion, and the experience of being without any real direction. Why? Because you're constantly fighting an invisible fight.

A perpetual internal brawl with the automatic, subconscious machinery that you are. Or least that you have become.

> *"Man is condemned to be free; because once thrown into the world, he is responsible for everything he does. It is up to you to give life a meaning."*
> *—Jean-Paul Sartre*

The reason I include this Sartre quote here is to highlight a really important aspect of what it is to be a human being. First, when he says we are "responsible for everything" we do, that works both ways. As an example, "it's not my fault" is a position one takes from a place of determining who is at fault. One is, in fact, being responsible for declaring who and who is not at fault.

Whatever you get lodged in there will also get applied to life as it happens in the future.

That's basically why a lot of your adult life feels like you're caught in an emotional Groundhog Day. Your fears? Yep, based on your past. Your hopes and dreams? Reactions to your past. Your rules or expectations or standards? Your past. And on and on and on.

You don't get stuck with just the events. You get stuck with what you said to yourself about them. A mental tattoo. Except every time that internal work of art gets exposed, you get the flood of emotions, characteristics, and logic that come with it.

Which is what makes it all so fucking personal.

And it bleeds into everything you do. Including your idea of what makes a good/bad/indifferent parent.

It's important that you begin to understand this in terms of your own children too or you'll become yet another walking-on-eggshells kind of parent, too terrified to move or speak for fear of what those little minds will be left with and the dread of discovering that it will eventually all be your fault.

We need to free ourselves from this narrative.

05

A FRESH PERSPECTIVE

Let me say this again in very plain terms for you. You are not shaped by the past itself. You are shaped by what you said to yourself (and continue to say to yourself) *about* that past.

Now of course you had (and have) no in-the-moment sense of doing such a thing, but you did do it and you still are doing it. It's all reactionary. An instantaneous mental record, emotionally wired to protect yourself. Your formative years are about building a reality of your mind and at the same time putting together the kind of you that can handle this stuff in the future.

The only difference between then and now is that in your past it was all new and now it's just old triggers being set off. You added significance then and you're doing it still.

It makes sense too, especially for a young mind. A child keeping track and building a picture for life would seem critical to survival, right? But it comes with a very natural and logical consequence. By a relatively young age that script becomes the background for the stage play called your life. It's the landscape of all that you do and don't do, never questioned, always present, always the same. You're now going around in life as a radar for all it represents. The foreground of your life is constantly being illuminated by what's still churning in the background.

All of your strategies as a parent are acted out against this already existing backdrop and it's so far back there you have been oblivious to it. Playing out the same little vignettes of life over and over, occasionally changing the actors and audience, but it's just the same fucking tired, dog-eared script being regurgitated day after day. It still sounds like you, smells like you, feels like you, looks like you, and acts like you no matter the situation. And wherever you go, the story continues.

Let that sink in.

How much longer can you continue following this narrative for life? Can you see the damage of living life this way? What do you think all of this is doing in the background either while you attempt to raise your own kids or be one to your parents?

Now, before you slink into a life-sucking ooze of self-pity, guilt, shame, or whatever else your little heart can muster . . . stop right there. That's not what this is. This is an exercise in self-realization. An awakening of sorts and sure, while there may be some residue from the process, your job is to steady yourself here.

How you relate to anything is always from a certain perspective, a viewpoint. If you want to change how you feel about a certain thing or person, you have to be willing to consider some other viewpoint. A different truth.

In other words, be open to changing your fucking mind!

Regardless of where you are in your race to the end, you can either stop using the past as a reason for doing what you are doing (and that means NEVER using it to justify yourself OR demean anyone from it) or you can shift how you now see it, just as I did.

A Hard Look at Self

How in the hell could I justify who I had become and expect people to understand me or, at the very least, make me a little more room for what I was dealing with as an adult, while by the same token, denying the people who had given me life the same compassion?

I mean isn't it just the same trauma but a different day? How could I, in all seriousness, treat my past like it was the tragedy of the ages while conveniently ignoring the idea that I may not be the only one who has gone through something?

Each of my parents had to deal with something in their childhood, and that shit followed them right into my childhood. Don't get me wrong, they were trying. But like a lot of people, life was a struggle. And they dealt with their struggles in the way that many, many people do—they acted like they were over it, but it just kept manifesting in their lives over and over. A real-life game of Whac-A-Mole. As a kid, on the surface and seeing from my eyes, it just looked like selfishness and hopelessness and anger and chaos. Looking back now it was all just survival, and survival is rarely pretty and I was right in the middle of it all.

And so were they.

I'll never throw my parents under the bus for how my childhood went, and believe me, I had plenty of evidence built up to do so, which I took advantage of repeatedly for much of my adult life. Until I awoke to who I had become. And when I confronted *that* person, it was an image I just did not care for in that bathroom mirror anymore. I was sick of me, and it all had to go if I was to reinvent what I was using my life for.

I was a blamer and complainer and stuck in an ordinary life of zero inspiration or any real sense of personal accomplishment. Trapped in my own cage that I now had to get the fuck out of.

It took a lot of thinking and immersing myself to get to this point. I had to get out of the addiction for seeing the world through only my eyes, my situation, my pain, my story, and the life I thought I should have had.

I had to use my brain to get free. And examining these pivotal moments from my story through *their* eyes made a massive difference in my ability to do just that.

I *got* them and in the process I got free. And so can you.

Which is why you may notice I'm not saying how any of that stuff *made* me feel. That's a phrase you will *never* hear me say anymore. That shit just doesn't belong in my vocabulary.

Why? Because language is important. I always come from the singular perspective of *I feel* because I'm unwilling to transfer the power of my feelings to someone or something else. I feel the way I do because I feel the way I do. That's it, nothing more, nothing less, and it's always the case.

I raise my children this way too.

And if I don't like the way I feel, I'll do whatever it takes to shift that experience until I feel differently. The world doesn't have to change to make me feel better. I got that shit handled. Sometimes that includes allowing myself the good grace to feel even the most negative of feelings instead of struggling to make it go away. How I feel is no one else's job, no one else's responsibility, I own it and I love living life as that owner because I'm always in charge of my emotions, moods, hooks, triggers, and whatever else arises in this skin bag from one day to the next.

I'm not saying it's an easy game to play but it's sure as hell the right one. And it's the one I played in reinventing my relationship with my mom. I completely let go of the character she had become in my story and took on the practice of seeing her through the contours of *her* story, not mine.

Suddenly I could love her for her journey, not her mistakes.

I asked questions, I got interested, I told her how much I loved her and appreciated her. I repeatedly thanked her for the gift of life, which, if you know anything about many Scottish people, was a fucking weird thing to talk about. But I did it anyway. Because I'd much rather be weird about how much I love someone than just about anything else in the world.

Fuck the weirdness, screw the discomfort, shower those people with your undeniable capacity to love them.

Did she change? Fuck no. But she didn't have to. After decades of devoting myself to all the ways I thought she should be different, I finally realized I was the one who needed changing. So I did.

And with all of that came a capacity to put myself into perspective. I now neither minimize nor exaggerate my feelings. There's no additional drama, no blame, no excuses or suppressing of self. But it still takes consciousness. I need to be aware of that automatic desire to point to the world or other people to explain how I am. And put it to rest.

My story about my parents now? They both loved me to their absolute limit, and I fucking turned out. They did what they did, they didn't do what they didn't do, and everything else is just bullshit as far as I'm concerned. I'm alive and changing lives and that's a gift I could never repay them for, the gift of life and of making a difference.

And, like me, you'll need to notice yourself too. And adjust.

A little addendum to this piece. If you're someone who feels like you've dealt with this and currently sum up your parents with "they did the best they could with what they had" . . . that ain't it.

And the reason that ain't it is because we're *all* doing the best we can with what we have in any given moment and that will be the case forever and a day. You're not better than they are, you're not more advanced than they are or floating high above the poor souls on some existential skateboard like fucking Marty McFly.

As a species, we are, we were, and we always will be struggling with the notion of what it is to be a human being, and the greatest thing you can ever do is start to see that as a universal truth rather than something that doesn't apply to you because you did the fire walk a few times and feel like you've exorcised your teenage demons.

You don't need to turn your parents into your children to transform your relationship to them, you only have to start seeing them as human beings and, like all human beings, they have a past, some of which you don't know and may never know. You should be aware that that past is still playing out in their life as an adult. Just as it has with you.

What if your parents are dead or if you did not know them? The same principles apply, no matter how much or how little you knew of them.

By having a better understanding of and compassion for your parents and how they were raised, it will also make you a better parent to your own kids.

Think you way through. Getting out of your story begins by seeing it from different perspectives, and sometimes just realizing yours is not the only one can be enough in the absence of the gory details.

The short of it is, you have to become bigger than the details of whatever past you have attached yourself to. To take a grander perspective, a philosophical stance, to pull back when the way of life up until this stage has been to zero in, to obsess, and to hang on to all that we have glued our souls to.

> *"Life is really simple, but we insist on making it complicated."*
> —Confucius

Playing the Right Game

Okay, we've uncovered the shit from your past, the traumas from your childhood, and now you're wondering, Gary, how do I keep from passing that shit down to my kids?

One of the biggest things you'll ever have to acknowledge is your ultimate inability to truly impact the outcome of your own child. I mean sure, you can flat out love 'em and insist on this behavior over that one, family customs, values, faith, or philosophy, but even then, haven't you seen, even with all that in place, a young person will still more than likely just head off in their own direction anyway?

We explain it away with this reason or that, poor education or bad influence or something they inherited from the black sheep of the family. Some parents become wracked with guilt or shame; others turn their back or uneasily "accept" the path their kid is taking.

Then there's the worry . . . oh my, the worry.

And if genetics is still wrestling with some of the vital questions of nature vs. nurture, I think we can safely put to bed whichever you think may be the answer here.

Is there a little chance you know a smidgen of a notion that we just might not have a fucking clue what we're doing? That we're playing the game we think we're supposed to be playing but in fact it's another game entirely?

"To the As-Yet-Unborn, to all innocent wisps of undifferentiated nothingness: Watch out for life. I have caught life. I have come down with life. I was a wisp of undifferentiated nothingness, and then a little peephole opened quite suddenly. Light and sound poured in. Voices began to describe me and my surroundings. Nothing they said could be appealed."

—Kurt Vonnegut Jr.

BREAKING THE WAVE DOWN

Life hits us like a wave.

A relentless, seething wall of chaos and confusion that has no interest in gently kissing the shoreline to simply then depart. Life rages through our fragile innocence, sweeping mercilessly and violently inland to pursue the rich harvest of youth and absorb all that it touches.

It consumes possibility and leaves resignation and cynicism in its wake. Until there is no "you" left. Only the aftermath. The counterfeit you. The person you had to become to make it through the storm then and forever thereafter. An inauthentic self.

We call all of that a childhood. Even those of you with sparkly magical childhoods don't escape unscathed. And from those remnants we set out to become adults, partners, spouses, mothers, or fathers. Living in rebellious reaction to, or struggling to stay in alignment with, all that came and went in those early years of life.

And while that may be true, the work to be done here, your part in this requires you to begin to see your past in terms of a process rather than the unchanging, tired old fable it has become in your head. To that end, what we'll examine over the next couple of chapters is how development through childhood and adolescence sets up what our life becomes about.

Life moves in a forward momentum—from the innocence of infancy, to the awakening of early childhood, to the building of our persona as we grow. Like a wave, it creeps and flows and shapes and eventually takes over. Takes over who or what? It takes over you and ultimately your life span.

In fact, everything that gets wrapped up in this wave is essentially what your life becomes about, and it all happens in the first twenty years of your existence. Everything you are organized around at this point in your life, regardless of your current age, was set up in those first twenty. If you're forty right now, you are twenty years deep into a game that was twenty years in the making.

So let me lay out the road map such that you at least may be able to understand where your situation is currently located.

Keep in mind that this is a framework and is set up for you to comprehend something fundamental that not only went down with you but that will with your children too. This construct is to within a year or two on either side and applies to your little angel, whether their behavior is currently straight out of the latest Disney princess movie or the bloody carnage from the director's cut of *Deadpool*.

I'm breaking this wave down into three easy-to-recognize parts that are roughly birth to age seven, seven to fourteen, and fourteen to twenty. This chapter will explore the first phase, and we'll look at the others in the next. Don't get hung up on the ages here either. Again, keep thinking of this like an evolving flow.

This is less about what they're doing and a whole lot more about what's going on in their head. You went through this and so will they.

The idea here is to give you a sense of where they (and you) are. You may well see that you're dealing with a largely universal human experience rather than a unique or personal one.

Ready? In we go!

The First Flood

You are not born "you."

You become the person you have become over a period of time.

Most personal development is built around the idea of improving or "unbecoming" some or all of that. All of this is pretty damn useless without understanding how the whole thing works.

In this case we're looking at what I call "the first flood." This is where it all starts. A human being's journey from a nothing to a something. When you are born, you are an opening, a possibility for life to take shape.

What does that mean? Start with the idea that in your earliest years, you have no real sense of a self, no idea of what the world is, and certainly no real filter to deal with other human beings either. You're a little nothing, spinning in fascination and thirsty for discovering everything that was going on around you, all the while, under the surface, building to become the something you are now.

> ### "Everything was beautiful, and nothing hurt."
> *–Kurt Vonnegut Jr.*, Slaughterhouse Five

Then things changed, step by step, situation by situation, one drama upon another, pain points drawn in the sands of your mind to remind you of who is who and what you'll need to avoid.

But there's a drawback in this initial phase of life.

Your ability to recollect is still in its formative stage, which is why most people have little more than hazy pictures in their mind's eye when attempting to recollect their infant years. Sure, they might be able to conjure up one patchy vignette or other, but there is no sense of time, of the bigger picture, it's all me, me, me in moments of life. And so it should be, because this is the phase where you start awakening to the idea of a "me."

There is no past, no future, it's all imagination, wonder, and full self-expression wrapped up in the present moment. But the wave is persistent, and with its ever-expanding presence comes the one skill human beings require to figure life out: language. Not speaking per se but rather we begin to use language to capture life.

We start to grasp language long before we can speak it.

With language comes the ability to capture things mentally. What is a chair before we learn what it's called? What about water or the sky or a foot or a cup?

Infants can often point to these things before they can accurately say them. I mean, of course, someone had to say that word over and over for them to connect the dots but nonetheless the ability to recognize "something" as "that thing," fusing the word to the item, arises with early language.

Popular science indicates that the average human being can recollect memories from about two and a half years of age but begins connecting words to things at about nine months.

So what? Well, I'll deepen this as we go, but the connection between things and language doesn't just stop with the fucking table and curtains. It extends all the way out to situations, to people, to emotions and behaviors. Language is invasive; it captures and fastens itself to the nothingness of the universe, where we derive meaning and purpose and understanding. With the expansion of language comes the growth of knowledge but also, significantly, the ability to recollect.

Your memories are housed in language. Read that again. Think.

"BUT WHAT ABOUT MY EMOTIONS, GARY?!!!!"

I was getting there . . .

Here's a wee quote I love to hang with from time to time.

> *"Language is the house of being. In its home human beings dwell."*
> *–Martin Heidegger*

You don't live *with* language. You live *in it*, and how you *be* is interwoven in that language. Stop here and think about this. You, right now, live in a construct of language, and your entire experience of being you, of being alive is a function of those words that make up the bricks and mortar of that house.

Everything you think, everything you say, hear, or read. All of it in language and all of it deeply intertwined with emotions, reactions, and feelings.

I often point people to their "story" for evidence of this. Write out your life story. That's the house you live in. Word for word, emotion by emotion, knitted together psychologically, neurologically, physiologically, your entire sense of self wrapped in the everyday language you use, a burdensome structure of pain and distress and loss and desire and whatever else made the cut.

So just change the words? Rewrite the story? Fuck no! We'll get into this later, but for now just hang with this concept of language and emotions.

This isn't a situation of feel first and the words come along to describe how you're feeling.

As an adult human being, the words you automatically use in an instant of time are arising *as one* with the emotions connected to them. When you speak or think about your passions, what do you experience? Passion. If you speak or think of regret, what do you experience? Regret. Same with hate, love, resentment, frustration, and every other emotional state that rattles your teeth daily. You instantly recognize and experience emotions in the words that fall out of your mouth or scamper across the surface of your thoughts. Your emotional state arises in the language you use to describe yourself, how you describe others, how you describe anything.

While what I'm saying here may be revolutionary to you, there's quite a body of evidence in academia for what I am proposing. Like this from the work of Lindquist, MacCormack, and Shablack:

According to the psychological constructionist Conceptual Act Theory (CAT), an instance of emotion occurs when information from one's body or other people's bodies is made meaningful in light of the present situation using concept knowledge about emotion. The CAT suggests that language plays a role in emotion because language supports the conceptual knowledge used to make meaning of sensations from the body and world in a given context.[1]

There is one caveat to this, which I've explained in other books.

There are those that believe, "think happy thoughts, live a happy life," which, apart from the off-putting,

---

1 K. A. Lindquist, J. K. MacCormack, and H. Shablack, "The Role of Language in Emotion: Predictions from Psychological Constructionism" (Chapel Hill: Carolina Affective Science Laboratory, Department of Psychology, University of North Carolina, 2015).

sugary Goody Two-shoes-ness of the quote, just does not line up and in fact is a particularly naïve examination of the subject. The one thing that holds emotions and language together is belief. Whatever you believe to be true is unquestioned. And those beliefs and emotions are lovers in the recesses of your subconscious, all wrapped in language.

It's hardly a massive leap in logic to begin to see the importance of language not only in early life but also for the entirety of a human being's existence because what you say and how you feel are one, and infancy is where this profound connection begins to take shape.

So if you're someone who has children under the age of roughly seven, they are slap bang in the middle of the first flood. That initial ontological wave of life that hits all human beings. If your kids are older, this will help you understand what they've already gone through.

You're getting a sense of what's going down here but what about in the mind of that little one? What's happening there with the accumulation of language and with it an ever-increasing ability to recollect?

Well, let's take it back a wee bit to say between nine and twelve months.

Have you ever witnessed a little one gaze at themselves in a mirror?

If you could speculate what's going on in their mind, do you think they recognize that reflection? If not, what are they interacting with?

See if you can muster up enough imagination and start to think about this with the eyes and ears of someone experiencing people and life for the first time. It's all amazing, scary, fun, filled with laughter and frustration and whatever wide range of emotions and feelings you can care to assemble on any given day. This is when we engage with our curiosity, and exploration is at the very front of that little mind. It's also when we start gathering language to articulate how we feel and what we are seeing.

This is the phase of life when "I" begins to take shape and with it the arising of an internal conversation that will last a lifetime. That little one is putting together the words that will allow them to connect that reflection they see in the mirror with their personal experience. And with those words . . . emotions.

And memories.

In the following weeks and months, you may well begin to see the early signs of a persona take shape. That cute little personality that's coming to the fore has a purpose, it's not just to make the big time on your Instagram feed. That first surge of life not only compels that little one to become aware of itself but also to sow the seeds of who they will have to be to counter whatever that early life throws at them.

As a parent you're just so enraptured by *who* they are becoming you cannot quite see *why* they are becoming. And the *why* is absolutely everything.

Let's make this crystal clear. Think back to your own early years. What is your earliest memory of trying to overcome something? Was it in kindergarten or school? Perhaps it was at home or while on vacation or playing in the yard.

Perhaps you were scolded or singled out, maybe you saw your parents arguing or you failed at something. Think. What is your earliest memory of having to overcome something or someone?

Most people can remember this early case of overcoming because it was so important in that young mind. Even with a good memory, you can't remember everything in your childhood, but you certainly remember *some* things. Start with the idea that those things are not random. Pay attention to the things you remember; they are useful information. Regardless of what you think of them now, they were significant to you at the time. So they stuck.

And they still stick.

And they became watershed moments. Events that changed you. Points from which you never returned.

Leading by Example

I can easily recollect a moment when I was three or four years old when I witnessed my parents in a blazing argument. I don't think this was the first time they had argued, but this one is the one that jumped out at me. I mean, I *guess* they had argued before, but there was something unique about this situation. And just like you and your memories, there is a hazy recollection of *some* details, but what sticks most was how I felt while watching the two most important people in my life shred each other for what seemed like an eternity but most likely could be measured in minutes.

There was the obvious shouting and screaming. I recall necks stretched, strained by voices seeking the space to be heard between breaths, gasping for air above the chaos with arms flailing, fingers aimed in the direction of their vitriol, eyes bulged, faces crimson with anger and threats of leaving and name calling, who is right, who is wrong, on and on and on. While the specifics of what was said are completely lost on me, I was clear, in that moment of my life, that this was an upset like I'd never seen before.

It stuck out. And it stuck with me.

Now as an adult, I'm not wandering around in constant reflection of that moment in my life, but given all of the work I have done on myself, I am clear that this was a formative yarn in the collective fabric that eventually became my story.

"An argument? A fucking argument became your story?"

No.

Just like you, I wasn't impacted by the thing itself but rather how I *felt* when it happened. The experience of myself that I could not overcome in that instant is what stuck. I changed and there was no going back.

How did I feel?

Weak. I'm weak.

I remember saying the word "stop." I don't recollect if I shouted it or screamed it or whispered it. What I do remember is that the conflict continued anyway. I just stood there. Watching. Unraveling.

I could not halt that sense of "weak" tighten its grip on my sense of self. I had no sense that what was washing over me was in fact taking over me. But there was an undeniable something about myself that shouldn't be. A newly discovered flaw. A defect or deficiency. It wasn't that I felt weak in the moment and never again. This was something that would resonate throughout my entire life forever after.

Occasional but regular revisits, not to the incident but rather to the experience. Particularly in moments of pressure or catastrophe.

And now, in that tiny three- or four-year-old head, I realized my powerlessness, I had words now inextricably linked to feelings and my sense of self. I obviously couldn't stop what was happening in that boxy orange and brown living room. I could only stand in paralyzed awe of this cacophony of human strife, frozen by my personal crisis and inability to do something, *anything* to change what I was seeing. But I couldn't. But this isn't about immaturity or a lack of development, I was only three or four years old after all, but rather this was a full-blown existential crisis erupting in that little head.

This was the end of innocence. There was life before that point and life after, but it just wasn't the same.

And that's how this shit goes down for people. For some it's big and traumatic and cruel; for others it's subtle and seemingly meaningless. Which is why this obsession with analyzing our every minuscule action for fear of what effect it may have on our children is basically bankrupt. We do not all have the same past, but we all come away with our own BS, which is why there needs to be less focus on the incidents and more on what you took from them.

I get it, though, after a lifetime of associating the incidents with the residual emotions and triggers, it seems really hard, maybe even disrespectful or cold to separate them, but separate them you must.

There is so much addiction to the incidents of your past, what happened, what should have happened instead, what they did, what they failed to do when none of that is what has you hooked, no matter what you have come to believe about any of it. Change your mind, anyone?

The real problem is understanding what you are now left with and what you did with that between then and now.

"It is one thing to show a man that he is in an error, and another to put him in possession of the truth."
—John Locke

For me, what was beginning in that moment when I felt powerless was the origin of the black hole that all human beings must live with. The one that we can become so embroiled in, we'll waste a lifetime trying to fill. It took me forty years of living to finally connect the dots for myself and embrace a life of authentic self-expression.

A life free from the past. And I didn't have to blame anyone or cut anyone out to do it.

We'll get to that for you too here.

But in *that* moment there were just three human beings locked in a flashpoint of time, each reacting to a turmoil of their own internal creation, all struggling to be heard or acknowledged or seen or comforted in this all-too-real situation of life.

What is your flashpoint? What moment do you remember so clearly as the one that opened your eyes to what was going on and how to survive it?

My parents and I were all lost in a mishmash of our own thoughts and emotions, hijacked by a brain that was completely absorbed with surviving the occasion, and if and when you can begin to see your own past in a similar way, you can really start to understand why blame is such a corrosive and unnecessary component of anyone's past.

We're all just trying to make it. And that solitary pursuit is where many a dream goes to die.

Everyone is fighting to get to the future while real treasure is right here, but I'll expand on this later when we start to take on what it looks like to be a parent with all of this insight.

For now, let's continue opening up this notion of the wave.

"When childhood dies, its corpses are called adults and they enter society, one of the politer names of Hell. That is why we dread children, even if we love them. They show us the state of our decay."

—*Brian Aldiss*

THE SURGE OF CYNICISM

AND THE FINAL FLOW

As life creeps ever stronger, ever deeper, evermore consuming and dangerous in the mind of a child, it is the natural way of things for all human beings to build the kind of psychological armor they will need to protect them against all changes and perceived threats long into the future.

Decisions set in stone, never questioned, always honored.

But they do not come without cost. In this process, many human beings lose touch with their innate ability to love, to be vulnerable, to be brave, settled, and happy. It's all buried under years of calloused thought, behavior, and fucked-up logic.

When people say "I'm just the way I am," it's the above they are referring to. What they fail to realize is that their senses of authentic self, real self-expression, and wisdom are buried underneath all of that.

Childhood is designed to produce a "you," and your job as an adult is to understand that after the fact, not during. You can't see it during because you're so deep in it. As a parent, the more you are able to see this with you own children, the less likely you are to panic on or distort the process.

As a parent, you're really only participating in the ride, not driving it, no matter how much you want it to be different.

You have your rules and values and whatever other colors you add to life but at the same time you need space to see and experience this process for what it is. A miracle. If I can offer you any "advice" it's to create as much room in your life and to stay out of the process as much as possible.

I'm well aware that's trickier than just about anything you've ever done in your life because you still need to guide; influence; protect; and, most of all, love this human being with all you can muster under every circumstance. But the point remains. Less force, more space.

This next assault of the wave can be a real tearjerker for some parents and, like everything in this book, your parents witnessed this with you, you'll see it in your own kids, and they will observe it with theirs.

This is where the cracks begin to change the shape of your safe little bubble of existence.

The Big Switch

> "When a child first catches adults out—when it first walks into his grave little head that adults do not always have divine intelligence, that their judgments are not always wise, their thinking true, their sentences just—his world falls into panic desolation. . . . And the child's world is never quite whole again. It is an aching kind of growing."
> —*John Steinbeck*, East of Eden

I think if there was ever a group of words that captures this phase of the wave so eloquently, this quote may be the most accurate and poignant of them all. We are entering the chapter of every human being's life where their fundamental role in the game of their own existence begins to shift. And this change is a massive one.

This wave is where we experience an ontological break from the world we had been in. Basically, that's a feature of every wave. A disconnect. The first seven years or so are about curiosity and wonder, where there is no distinction between you and life because your experience is that you *are* life. You are the center of it all and there are no seams, no breaks, no separations between you and everything going on around you. You're connected with everyone and everything and at one and dancing in the now with no sense of anything but the complete awe of being alive.

Then, in a moment of time, in a momentous switch, you realize you're a "you."

Not a perfect, nothing-wrong-in-the-universe kind of you but rather one where you have witnessed your own personal failure. An emotional shortcoming.

I've heard it said that a human being spends the entirety of their life trying to get back to that very first experience of being. The first wave. It certainly explains a lot of our pursuits and subsequent behavioral flaws.

This next phase sees that flaw in others. Innocence will be replaced with something else: cynicism.

That's right, roughly between ages seven and fourteen is where a human being discovers their massive muscle for cynicism.

And this shift to cynicism is a pivotal one because this is the time when a human being stops understanding themselves as the involved *player* of this game and jumps over to the stands to become the primary *observer* of it. Some parents recognize this switch happen in their children. Not quite what happened but that clearly *something* had happened. That their kid was somehow different. Most just put it down to "growing up" because they're not keyed into what's actually altering in front of their eyes.

It's in this existential break, where the safe little cocoon of a human being's thoughts and feelings and emotions becomes fractured, never to return, that their world has changed decisively and permanently. And this cynicism sticks with them into adulthood. It can be hard to spot with a young human being, but many parents will testify to the shift. Noticeable yet untraceable.

Now don't get me wrong, as an adult you can still reach for the positivity juice when you need to but at the root of it all is your often denied cynicism. Many people cannot even be with the idea that underneath all of their bluster and bullshit lies a deep-rooted suspicion, a tranche of to-the-bone pessimism that exists in all of us but, if you look, it doesn't take much to discover. If you're honest.

Many times, when I present people with some kind of alternate possibility for their life, they immediately respond with why that's not possible for them. Like it sounds good but it's either too hard or too simplistic, or not applicable in their situation.

Cynicism.

The truth of it is, as adults we are all merely observers of life. I mean, we talk like we're in the game, like we're playing, we're this or that; hell, it even *feels* like we're in the fucking game! But you only have to look at Twitter,

Facebook, Instagram, nights out with friends, at home with family, or shooting the shit with co-workers . . . conversations filled with our observations and insights, our opinions and outrages, and all from the perspective of the onlooker. Finding common topics with others to find some sense of belonging in the chaos of being alive.

Playing the game of life is when you put yourself at risk, when you forgive, express your love, anywhere you expose yourself to humans' kryptonite: the potential judgment of others.

And all the stuff you're cynical about but have no sense that you can change, you'll learn to live with. You'll live alongside it, occasionally upset by it or double down on your attempts to prove you are victorious over it, but there it remains.

Let's put it this way: you were not born cynical, but you certainly were born to become that way, and this second wave is where that cynicism begins to emerge.

But we come out of each phase changed. Changed and then into the next one. Yet when we're "in it" we have no sense of such a thing. Because we're busy.

Life is happening fast, life is coming at us and we're ducking and diving and interpreting it, but the wave just keeps coming. And that's how it is for your kids at this age and how it was for your parents when they were growing up too.

The truth of it is, it has always been less about what happened and more about what each person did with what happened, which begs the very next question.

What in the hell do you do with all of this as a parent? I mean, where do you think that cynicism your child is discovering is most likely to be directed?

At you. Or your spouse.

The observation takes hold, the cynicism emerges, and a certain "truth" begins to take shape in the eye of the observer. Now if you think about it, being cynical is a necessary component for being a human being; we require a certain "dry eye" to draw down on a world that could potentially fuck us over.

Cynicism makes developmental sense. It's normal. But it also begins the first break between child and parent.

Your hypocrisy will no longer go unnoticed, even the little things that you don't think matter or are irrelevant will show up on their radar. Your double talk, your little white lies, bending of integrity, and subtle (or obvious) manipulations will become increasingly clear to them. The stuff you've been pretending to yourself about, the indiscretions and pretenses, the indulgences and lies are all now on the table and you'll have a choice to make, but we'll get into all of that soon enough.

I can't say this in any way other than this: they are on to you in a manner that many parents become uncomfortable or defensive about. And while we're on the subject, it's fair to remind you that when you were a child, you could well have gone down this pathway with your own parents and no amount of evidence, defense, or justification from them would have changed the direction you had taken. Stew in that for a minute or two.

As your child experiences this shift, your job as a parent is never to try to fix something. Why? Because there is nothing wrong. Play the long game. This was supposed to happen. Did you seriously think that chubby little ball of fun and energy you used to swaddle and soothe to sleep would stay the same all the way through life?

Sure, they're still a kid, they encompass much of that same innocence and joie de vivre they so easily expressed as a toddler. They might still like a cuddle and a laugh and all the other things, but you, as the adult in the vicinity, need to be aware that they either have changed, or they will be doing so soon. It's normal, and it's okay.

It's about them now.

For once, don't make this about you. This is about what is going on in their heads now.

I know that seems obvious, but so much of what you are seeing in your children is about them, their reality, what they are dealing with, even when it includes their oh-so-close-to-the-bone observations about you or your spouse.

As the song goes, the times they are a-changing, and it's perhaps your big opportunity to move with them.

> *"The only way to make sense of change is to plunge into it, move with it and join the dance."*
> *—Alan Watts*

The Final Flow

This is it, the final flow, the last scene of a childhood play with some profoundly serious consequences.

> *"I don't believe one grows older. I think that what happens early on in life is that at a certain age one stands still and stagnates."*
> —*T. S. Eliot*

Some people might find this quote a little hard to be with.

Others can immediately identify with all that it brings to mind. No matter where you are on the range, try this on. You are the natural progression of the adult you decided you would have to be during this last phase.

If you take a few steps back, it's not too challenging to imagine why this is often the trickiest of all phases to navigate and usually for everyone involved. Not always, but usually. We'll define this phase as occurring between the ages of fourteen to twenty.

But, just like the other phases, this one is completely necessary from an evolutionary standpoint for all human beings. Unfortunately, this can also be the phase from which some families never quite recover.

While research is somewhat limited, the general consensus is that in these years of the wave is when young people tend to cut themselves off from their family unit. Sometimes permanently.

I know many of the readers of this book will be able to recollect this phase of life most clearly. Many of you talk about this time as a defining period, and for some the shift that happened here dealt a fatal blow to the thing you call family.

For many this was a flammable, unsteady phase of life. It begins with a burning desire to do things differently, for a young person to head off and live their own life. Rebellion is common, sometimes under a cacophony of noise, sometimes in the quiet of thoughts and dreams, but it's not hard to see its roots in the cynicism of earlier days.

As a parent, here's what you need to understand: there must be a break. Otherwise your kids would be living with you until the end of time. No matter how much you love your kids, nobody wants that.

As the child of a parent, here's what you need to understand: this chasm had to be exposed, it quite literally had to happen. For both parties.

Whether you like this or not is irrelevant, and if you are still upset with how it happened, that's irrelevant too. This was always on like fucking Donkey Kong, and it's the one thing from many people's past that seems so freaking personal.

The point is, you're screwed until you understand.

Understand that you'll be chasing the ever-shifting shadows of circumstances or events trying to fix this thing or that, to pinpoint the "problem" when your eyes need to be firmly on the natural order of becoming an adult human being.

When a parent sees their child enter this next phase, the part we are calling "the final flood" and is often referred to as the "teenage years," there are so many physical and mental changes taking place it's hard to see the most important change of all.

Your child is now looking at a future without you in it.

Or, at least without you in it in the way you were before. You see, whether you like it or not, the family unit that was designed to protect, nurture, and incubate the child is about to end. It's about to become something else. Unfortunately, many parents struggle with this notion, just as much as their kids but for very different reasons.

As a young person, the most obvious thing to do is to push back against perceptions of authority and control that are keeping them from living their own life. All of this just feeds directly into the major weakness of almost all parents: fear.

Let me say this as plainly as possible: **all control is driven by fear.**

Are you getting this?

We all live with the illusion of control, and no situation captures this more dramatically than with our children. Now, of course, some people take their fear to almost theatrical lengths, scurrying after this thing or that, putting in layers of rules and practices and all to handle what is really going on in their head.

Fear. Fear of what? Usually some kind of perceived threat.

And this is a tremendous challenge for many parents with children in the fourteen-to-twenty age range.

It signals the end of an era. It's a heady mixture of sadness and frustration and vulnerability and panic like there's a change happening and there is absolutely nothing you can do to stop it. It's out of your control.

Some parents double down and are unfortunately only throwing fuel upon an already raging inferno of change. This is often the phase where parents actually experience their own little crisis because they are confronting the next phase of their own life and it's fucking intimidating!

Now, of course, you may have had parents who seemed to handle this very well, maybe even told you they were looking forward to life with you away at university or the military, or hell, maybe they went the entirely opposite way and threw you out!

If you were one of those kids of the latter and were forced to leave, you can bet your bottom dollar that was for one of two reasons, possibly both.

1. **The days of control were over, and this was your parents' last throw of the dice. They may be so dug in with that now, they cannot find a way back.**

2. **They never quite got over their own personal crisis about their youth and started to resent their adult life and with it everyone who was part of it. You included.**

I'm obviously making no excuses for either of these, but in my experience they are not to be underestimated in terms of their power to drive people in certain directions in their lives. Often with quite horrendous results.

Understanding is key here of course.

For any young person facing this phase, what is there to say about this that hasn't been said a gajillion times and smeared across every coming-of-age movie since James Dean first broke the mold in theaters with his performance in *Rebel Without a Cause*?

I say that fully in the knowledge that many would argue there is no such thing as "coming of age" and that we merely "age," but as we've seen here, these first years result in such a dramatic shift from infancy through our mid to late teens, the likes of which we will never experience again, I think it fair to say there's an end to an era that is incomparable to any other in our lifetime.

Your job at this point in the book is to finally embrace not only your own past as a process rather than a fable, but also to come to terms with the adults your own parents became from their process *and* the fact that your children are slap bang in the middle of theirs.

If your children are adults, well . . . now you know. Maybe there's a conversation you need to have to clean up some of the mess you made in their childhood.

As I said earlier: this is normal. Nothing is wrong, there's nothing to fix, even when your teenager never seems to listen to a word you say. This is a process they are working through, it's part of their development into a functioning adult, and your job is to help them through the process.

08

THE THREE HEIRLOOMS

There's a bit of a quandary here if you haven't noticed it yet, namely this: if you and I have based our parenting on what worked or didn't work from our own childhood, what worked or didn't work with how our parents did or didn't raise us, and now we're saying none of that is significant, then it begs the question what now?

Unfortunately, our obsession with how we *don't* want our children to end up is a massive diversion from the real issue. And while it's true that this is often the case in many other areas of life too, when it comes to our kids, we are primarily focusing on what we think we should avoid even though we've convinced ourselves we are doing what we think is "best."

We're avoiding them having our issues and hang-ups, or how the neighbors' kids turned out, or a vape problem, or emotional issues or getting left behind academically or bullied or . . . you get the picture.

Don't even get me started with your constant drive for them to somehow have the character traits you feel as if you don't have:

"You need to be more focused."

"You're too disorganized."

"You need to make friends."

Some people will quite literally tell their kids not to be like Mom or Dad. You'd be amazed at the number of people attempting to raise their children to be the kind of human being they have thus far failed at being. And in doing so, often repeat the failures of their own parents.

> *"Whoever fights monsters should see to it that in the process he does not become a monster. And if you gaze long enough into an abyss, the abyss will gaze back into you."*
> *—Friedrich Nietzsche*

In my experience, young people by and large really don't listen. I mean why the fuck should they? Most parents are hardly the radiant example of all that is good in humanity. And while they may not hear you, they do *see* you, and when your words don't match your actions, they can see right through your bullshit. As they are getting older you are getting by on ever decreasing levels of credibility with them.

For the most part, all that we think we are creating or getting done with our kids diverts us away from the kind of inquiry we really should be having.

If you keep doing what you're doing, what do *they* end up with?

We enforce this rule or that rule "in the name of" their safety. We insist on their commitment or hard work "in the name of" their success. We diminish their expression "in the name of" making sure they fit in and survive. All they hear is enforcing, insisting, and diminishing.

When it's all said and done, what kind of adults arise from the morass of a childhood, and what can you, as a parent, do about any of that?

On one hand, as we discussed earlier, you can *do* absolutely nothing about how your kids turn out, and it's our fascination with the idea that we somehow can that sends us off on some wild goose chase, searching for whichever list of dos and don'ts that will somehow see them turn out.

Ultimately all parents want the exact same thing: "I hope I don't fuck this up and that my kids somehow turn out."

Don't get me wrong, many, many parents end up doing exactly that, but take it from me, there's a point for every parent, either before that little one arrives, or in their first few days, weeks, months, or years, or in their teens, or their twenties, when they have to deal with a spine-bending weight from being visited by the specter of the potentially dark future that's yet to come.

The threat of getting this wrong is real.

And it's intimidating. Some parents are wrestling with that fear regularly, particularly those who struggle in their current circumstances. Divorce, health issues, separation, financial hardship, alcoholism, drug addiction, and death in the family are all examples of situations where parents become increasingly burdened by the job they have to do.

It's little surprise that many just surrender and wade their way through it on the raw, exposed fibers of their wits' end. We fail in the aftermath of parents who may have failed us, who were failed by their parents and their parents and their parents and on and on.

We may hope for better but that's just not enough.

Let's be honest: we're just not good at giving the equipment for life away. Some profess to having worked out their shit by the time their grandchildren arrive, but I usually put that down to an easing of the *press* on their sense of survival.

Everything's easy when life is easy. Including the little ones.

But none of that will help your kids much when it comes to stepping up and trying to raise their own family. They'll be as ill equipped as you've found yourself to be.

But it doesn't have to be that way.

A Chain Worth Keeping

I thought long and hard about what I wanted to gift my children.

Obviously this wasn't in terms of my favorite T-shirt or book or coffee recommendations to stand them in good stead for their adult life but rather the kind of guiding principles they could turn to long after I am gone.

I wanted my children to have something, a set of personal life skills, a range of talent for mastering their own humanity, but I absolutely knew none of it would make any difference for them if I did not first deal with how I was going to "give" them anything.

I mean, how do I give them something such as love or patience or any one of a number of the intangible tangibles we live our lives by?

Then it hit me: by living it myself. With no expectation or pressure that they follow suit. They either will or they won't, but as I am sure you will uncover for yourself, the kind of things I'm talking about here have real *impact* and not just with your kids but also with everyone else in your life.

Your parents included.

I have personally coached tens of thousands of people in my career in workshops, conferences, and groups all over the world. I've worked with people through all kinds of traumas, dramas, tragedies, you name it. I've heard it ALL over numerous continents, a multitude of cultures, and a smorgasbord of languages.

For eighty hours a week, thirty-three weeks of the year, week after week, month after month, year upon year I committed myself to delving into the darkness with people. Human beings laid bare, vulnerable, and determined to change. And they did.

Why am I telling you all of this?

I don't say anything here in a vacuum. I'm not anesthetized to what human beings are capable of. I am in no doubt as to the levels of cynicism, lying, cheating, hating, bullying, violence, intimidation, manipulation, and whatever other horrible and shameful things you may care to throw in the mix that human beings are capable of exacting upon one another.

Maybe you've done it, or it has been done to you. This is a harsh and cruel world at times. People do shit things to other people.

And your children will have to make it through all of it.

And sometimes our efforts to protect end up taking them in a direction we never anticipated. I go the other way. I don't want my children equipped with emotional survival skills. I want them to be bigger than life, to have a deep well of expression and an unmessable sense of self.

A robustness that's a match for the world and does not need them to look to anyone or anything to help them through it.

And so, through all of this coaching experience, I noted three things that continually caused people to fall. Three characteristics that, if they had mastered, would have seen them through just about every trial and tribulation of not only their young life but the rest of it too.

I call these three things "heirlooms" because that's exactly what they are. Three treasures that are at the center of everything we do here. Live by these and you can work through just about anything life cares to throw at you. Keep doing what you are doing and . . . well, we know how that turns out.

HEIRLOOM NO. 1: **BEING LOVING**

Love is the most obvious trait we would all like to see in our children. Who wouldn't want their kid to be someone who can enjoy the fulfillment and satisfaction of what love brings to their life? But as you and I know, it's all too easy to become hardened by life, to shut down, safety in isolation, a certain kind of freedom but in a box of our own making. A box strengthened by an unshakeable belief in the past.

Fuck that.

Being the parent here kind of forces us to deal with our own BS. If you are to *be* a full-blown demonstration of what it is to actually *be* loving, then where do you think would be the first place to look for evidence of such a thing?

Easy. All the places where there is currently something in the way of it.

Anyone can tell another they love them when the situation fits. Even the stingiest of hearts can come up for air from time to time as long as the occasion warrants it. Then there are those that throw the "L" word around like there's no tomorrow until it carries the same weight as the last bead of sweat on a butterfly's left bollock on a hot summer day.

For what it's worth, I love full out. To hell with the consequences. If you're in my life, I love you and there are no levels involved. I say it, I demonstrate it, I make it obvious too, no signals or mysteries to be solved, no languages to be understood. My love is bold, and I never use it to make you treat me differently either. That's called manipulation, my friend.

You do you and I do me and when it comes to me, love is everything.

If you're upset with me, I'll love you, if you don't want me in your life, I'll love you still, if you resent me or speak badly of me, look out . . . I still love you. I mean, we may not be best friends but my love for all people is at the very heart of everything I do, parenting included.

This isn't just a way of living for me. I am perfectly clear and aligned with the kind of human being I show up as in the lives of those around me. I am fully committed to being loving in a family, community, and world where everyone is a someone. And I am this for myself and all those people.

I refuse to entertain apathy and pain and suffering, but before you think I've been the one sucking down the positivity juice while writing this book, it's important that you realize there are many times in my day or week when being loving is the last thing on my mind. I am awakened to those dark crevices of my subconscious, those old patterns for seclusion and bitterness and hair triggers for being taken advantage of and yet I still show up. Because my commitment to being someone in this life is far greater than anything this bag of skin and bones can vomit from the past.

I take none of this lightly, but by the same token, I do not force it upon anyone. Love just is and so am I.

I truly feel the most important treasure I can hand to my children is to be a demonstration of what is possible in a world that's pulling for something else entirely. To be extraordinary when ordinary would just do.

HEIRLOOM NO. 2: **BEING FORGIVING**

"Forgiveness" is a word that gets thrown around a lot. It can also be a very challenging way of being to adopt because it is all too often in a fistfight with our most rudimentary human wiring.

In my experience, that's almost entirely down to a basic misunderstanding about what forgiveness is and what it isn't. Forgiveness does not mean what happened is suddenly "okay" and people have the freedom to turn around and do it all again. Forgiveness also does not mean things are back to the way they were; in fact, it often means things have changed irrevocably. But, by the same token, not necessarily for the worse either.

We are most likely to assign forgiveness to those we feel "deserve" it. That's not forgiveness, that's morality and therefore heavily laden with "right" and "wrong" and "good" and "bad" and yet another reason why we often cannot quite get our head around it.

Forgiveness, like love in its purest sense, needs no evidence for itself. It just is.

Forgiveness is when you let go of the desire to punish either yourself or another by holding onto an emotional position over something. It is quite simply the conscious choice to no longer punish.

In effect you are saying, "I am no longer willing to use my life to punish you for what you did or did not do."

I think most human beings can imagine some situation from their life where this may be a useful approach to take, but there is none more so than with yourself. To forgive yourself is to let go of the need or desire to dwell in something, to be unwilling to punish yourself for something you did or did not do.

But I'll let you into a little secret about those who cannot or will not forgive themselves.

On one hand there is a certain kind of nobility or admirable trait for those who hold themselves to account for their actions. The tribe, remember? Punishing yourself very often looks good to the tribe because it looks like you have learned your lesson and you can stay in the relative comfort and safety of the group. I mean, you are still being judged, but if you're heavy enough on yourself, you will likely start to garner sympathy.

"Oh, I'm a terrible person."

"No, you're not."

"YES, YES, I AM!!"

"No, you are not!"

"Okay, maybe you're right, I'm not so terrible after all."

Let's be honest here, we've seen little ones do this many times and it's a bit silly to think adults are not indulging it too, albeit in a slightly less obvious way.

So that's one major hidden aspect of it. Then there's the other. Indulging in self-blame gets you massively off the hook for two things.

1. **Being responsible for your current happiness. You can get back in the blame game, blame yourself, and hide from getting yourself on the hook for, oh, I don't know, joy?**

2. **You don't have to do shit about the future. No risk, no exposing yourself for what's next in your life, you can just hang out, spinning your fucking wheels and explaining your junk.**

Nice, huh?

As with lots of things in life, there's one little caveat: grief. If you are struggling with grief, you are unlikely to go straight to forgiveness. There are many ways to process grief, and it's something I distinguished in my book *Wise as Fu*k*. However, you will still have to face the prospect of forgiveness at some point in your process. That's okay, but at the same time, never just throw your arms in the air when it comes to handling grief. There are ways to do it, and if you are wrestling with it, the sooner you get started the better.

Now, again, you cannot "use" any of this to make your children be different. I like to call that "give to get," which is such a failed strategy for us as human beings, but some still insist on its hollow usefulness.

It's also completely inauthentic. Anytime you are saying or doing something so you can "get" something else is called a pretense. Pretending one thing (no matter how sincerely you may insist) to get something else is all just fakery bullshit. Not the real deal. Not genuine. Not authentic.

Simple, huh?

I sometimes admit to forgiveness as my personal superpower (I have a few). I use it all over the place, I forgive, I forgive, I forgive. I forgive me, I forgive you, I forgive them and them and them and all the while I am empowering myself, taking stock of what I'm up to, what I need to manage and forging the life of my fucking dreams.

The reality is I am completely and absolutely unwilling to trade my life for resentment.

If you want resentment . . . go ahead, it's all yours. I am a living, breathing expression of this in my home and in my life. I use the word "forgiveness" regularly with my wife, my children, my friends, and my team, and they all get to share their life with that kind of human being and, truth be told, I already see the fresh growth sprouts of forgiveness popping up with each of my three sons.

Forgiveness is the doorway to what is next. A grudge or resentment will see you never being able to pass through that door. It's an exchange. The past for the future. One or the other. Choose.

The future is filled with new levels of aliveness and possibility and adventure, all just waiting to be claimed as yours. The past? Been there, done that.

HEIRLOOM NO. 3: BEING SOMEONE OF INTEGRITY

Before I really studied the matter, I always understood integrity as something that is inseparable from being seen as a fundamentally "good" person. I was incorrect in that regard, so let's get some juice from the dictionary so we can break this down.

> **integrity**
> *noun*
>
> **adherence to moral and ethical principles; soundness of moral character; honesty.**
>
> **the state of being whole, entire, or undiminished: to preserve the integrity of the empire.**

Now, when you look at the first definition, it's easy to see why I, like most people, looked upon integrity like some form of moral fiber, which, truth be told, always seemed too fucking clean-cut for this old rocker in his younger days. To hell with that!

I was never much of a guy for chinos. More a leather pants and Carolina bike boots kinda dude. Anyhoo . . .

The main reason why that first distinction of the word is troublesome is down to the complete subjectivity of things such as ethics and morality. Both are fantastic subjects in philosophy but not what we're after here.

It's the second line that deserves our attention, namely *the state of being whole, entire, or undiminished.*

Hmmm . . . integrity as a *state of being*? I mean, a bridge can have structural integrity, right? You could say a bridge is in a state of being whole. Maybe your car or your roof or your television remote, for that matter. They are in a certain condition that allows them to function in service of their purpose, and if they were to downgrade in any way due to mishap or wear and tear, they would no longer have the kind of integrity that would allow them to continue reliably as they had done before.

Think of all the things in your home that you are tolerating, things that are breaking down, on their way out, taped up, roped together, missing one thing or another, but they still *kind of* work . . . right?

Yeah, but that's the problem. If you were sitting in your seat on an airplane and the pilot came over the intercom and said, "We'll be leaving in about five minutes. I have completed the checklist and we're kinda good enough to fly."

How long would you be sitting in that seat?

Now, I know that check engine light in your car or list of emails you need to get to might not be as deadly as the scenario I just painted, but everything you do has an impact. And when you are trying to get life done with a bunch of broken, incomplete, unfinished, half-arsed "stuff' strewn across the landscape of your life, is it little wonder you get burned out or overwhelmed from time to time?

So if we go back to the bridge as an example, if it started to structurally deteriorate, they will likely shut it down, make repairs (restore the integrity), and reopen as before. Bingo.

Except you're not a fucking bridge.

You're a person.

How does a person demonstrate a "state of being" whole?

The quick answer is their word. When someone consistently holds themselves to be who they *say* they are (as opposed to how they *feel* they are), you could say that is someone operating in a way that is whole and complete.

At some level, you already know this. This is that experience you have when you've done what you know to do in the way it was supposed to be done. Completing a report, going to the gym, eating what you're supposed to eat, staying calm in the storm, cleaning your car, it doesn't really matter the thing but rather your experience of being you. That state of being whole.

Where what you said and what you did were aligned. And your shit works.

And when you do not function that way, when you lose your temper or give up or lie or cheat, you are completely aware of that experience of yourself after the fact. You're not aligned with you.

And where your word doesn't match your actions. Shut down the bridge. Make the repairs. And get it back open and functioning the way it's supposed to.

How do you do that with your word?

If your word is simply a bunch of what you said you would do (it also includes what you *know* to do and what is *expected* of you and if you are going along in blissful ignorance of what is expected of you, that lacks integrity too), then your first real job here is to get clear about all of that.

As a father and a husband, I'm clear about what I said I would do, what I know to do, and also what I'm expected to do, and I fucking do all of it. Until I don't. Then I briefly shut down the bridge, be in communication with everyone impacted, and get myself straightened out.

I function *with* integrity. I do what I do like integrity matters to me because it does.

I'm not doing any of this in pursuit of perfection and I don't make myself wrong where I fail or sometimes reach with my promises a little farther than my calendar will allow me to go.

It's all good.

I live by a code where my life is a function of what I say, and the only real obstacle always comes back to my willingness to have my actions line up with that.

• • •

If I can show my sons love, forgiveness, and integrity, maybe not always perfectly, that may be the best thing I can give them as a parent.

I love them and the people in my life when I don't always "feel" like it. I forgive because I can, not because I should. And I live my life like what I say and what I do actually matter. No shadows, nowhere to hide. I do not excuse or justify my behaviors, I own them all, and with that approach I am bigger for it.

Just as you can be.

09

THE AUTHENTIC PARENT

I know many of you are really struggling with being a parent, and by my reckoning that also equates to some kind of struggle with being yourself.

In light of all we've been working on in these chapters, there is really only one way for you to be from here on out.

Authentic. Anything less would be a complete sellout.

If you've read my books or followed my work at all, you know I'm big on authenticity in all parts of life. And it is especially important when it comes to being a parent. Still, I recognize that "authenticity" is the fashionable word to use these days in the world of personal growth and development. Scattered lavishly across the entire spectrum of social media and whispered softly in the "new you" workshops and sweat lodges as the holy grail of human accomplishment, the ultimate goal of all that we do and need.

Unfortunately, it has also been grossly bastardized, overused, and waved as a flag of convenience to hide otherwise shitty behaviors.

"I'm being my authentic self" when complaining or throwing someone under the bus or gossiping or bursting the flimsy dam that's been holding back your resentment or anger is just NOT what it's saying on the can. Giving someone a piece of your mind is NOT authenticity, but it seems that no matter how you break this down for some folks, they'll just disagree and continue to justify imposing their upsets on the world.

And hiding behind that banner is the definition of inauthentic, i.e., NOT authentic at all.

Being your authentic self in this life will demand regular and consistent attention because you, like all human beings are hardwired for inauthenticity and you will habitually and without any real thought continue to be inauthentic. As an adult, you are heavily conditioned *not* to be yourself but instead continue to prance around the stage called life as the version of you that is most equipped to survive the spotlight, and while survival is on one hand a good thing, it's hardly a mode for all that a modern life presents us with.

And it's how you are raising your children right now. They'll do the heavy lifting but you're pointing the way.

I don't think it makes any real difference to use a word such as "authentic" without pulling it apart a bit so you can find out what it looks like for you. Let's start with the dictionary definition:

> **authentic**
> *adjective*
>
> **of undisputed origin; genuine.**

Seems pretty simple. Now, there is also an entry in the dictionary for the philosophical definition of authentic, and it goes something like this:

> **relating to or denoting an emotionally appropriate, significant, purposive, and responsible mode of human life.**

I think it's fair to say many people could explain their behavior as "emotionally appropriate" no matter how extreme it may get. That's mostly because we are by and large run by our emotions and they are invariably intertwined with a justification or two. Or ten. We explain ourselves rather than intervene because intervening takes effort and often exposes us to the risk of being judged by others. Real and imagined.

So we'll take the well-worn path of inauthenticity to protect and forward our sense of self. Except the only thing that gets forwarded is layer upon layer of inauthenticity. And thus life goes.

Let me lay down a marker here:

> **You are not authentic. You pretend, lie, hide, subvert, and manipulate just like everyone else.**

> **You are not the real deal because you cannot be until you confront all that you've hung onto.**

Although finally admitting that would be the first glimmer of authenticity for any human being.

So what are you? You are a version, a caricature, a product of a story decades in the making with traits and behaviors and repetitive emotional states with the upsets and triggers to match. You also have the personal strengths that this character would require to overcome the story in which it exists. And you are completely ensconced in the logic of it all.

None of which is you.

It's all just the "you" you have become bound to. When you begin to get into this line of thinking, it can really burst into your brain like a complete mindfuck, but what I am describing here is what many people encounter at a certain point in their lives. It's most commonly referred to as the "midlife crisis," but I prefer a much more accurate term: the bankruptcy of self.

If the first twenty years of life the wave is basically about determining what you are against as a human being and formulating the kind of you that you'll need to become to deal with it, the next fifteen to twenty years are about fighting that battle. The same battle. Over and over.

Then something happens.

Over time there's a gradual and undeniable realization of the fucking sham that your life is and the emergence of this question,

"How in the hell did I get *here*?"

Oh, boy. How many lives are ultimately ruined by the immediate answers thrown up by that inquiry?

Given that we exist in a culture of blame, the roulette wheel gets various spins, and wherever it lands, that's where the blame goes. After the blame there're the most obvious solutions, and off we go into what many people term their life reinvention when really it's just a change. Out of one pair of socks and into another.

A world where relief gets mistaken for freedom, where the blueprint for a new life is invariably taken straight out of the drawings of the first. Not new but rather just *different*, and while that seems like enough for most people, it's certainly not a life lived free from the constraints of whichever past they're trying to transform. Overcome, yes; transform, no.

Some of you are children of parents who faced this very thing. Some of whom stayed around; others left. Both can have an impact regardless.

You're One of Us

This leads us to a question that's very much overdue for every parent: what does it look like to be authentic as a parent?

Simple.

You tell the truth, and while that's the case for every area of your life, it's a critical aspect of being the kind of parent who actually makes a difference.

Now, of course, telling the truth as a parent doesn't mean you're burdening your children with every whine, drama, upset, or hardship you're struggling with, so let me set this up for you. Like a lot of what I say, this is something you really should be applying to every area of your life, not just your parenting. But here goes.

Before you mindlessly open the gaping cavity just below your nose, you should give full consideration to the kind of human being who will be listening: their maturity, their emotional scope, their integrity or behaviors, all of it. And when you do this, you are being responsible for whatever is about to fall out of your own mouth.

Unfortunately, as a society we are becoming so embroiled in our divisiveness we are giving less and less of a fuck about how we communicate or how it lands. So, we become irresponsible and let the chips fall where they may whenever we speak. And while you may defend your right to say whatever the fuck you want, I can't help but notice the irony of such a thing when the world in turn doesn't seem to give much of a fuck about you.

Who cares anyway? That's easy to say when your life is, for the most part, working.

There are two things I learned many years ago that continue to reap a bountiful harvest in terms of my happiness and peace of mind.

1. **Speak like your words mean *everything*.**

2. **Listen without making it mean *anything*.**

Seems simple enough, right? It is.

Start paying attention to what you are saying and to whom, and make sure your communications are heard as you intend. If you're struggling to make your point heard, start the conversation with "I can't seem to say this the way I want, so let me know if this sounds weird."

Stop trying to work out in your head your anxiety or nervousness or fear or whatever. Prepare the landing strip, as I like to say.

"I'm anxious about this so . . ." is a great place to start. Don't make a big deal of it but get the marker up in plain sight. You're opening people up to you, y'know, being authentic?

On the other side of that, whenever someone is communicating with you, you'll need to take a little bit more time catching yourself adding whatever interpretation.

Now, while all of this bears the hallmarks of responsible, authentic communication, there's obviously more to it when you are speaking with a six-year-old compared to a fourteen- or twenty-year-old, and while I'm usually hesitant to use examples from my own life, I'll indulge this a little right now because what I am about to share came to light when I began to embrace the idea of parenting my first son authentically.

As with every example, don't get caught up in the details but instead focus on the world that gets created here.

About ten years ago, I was spending multiple weeks on the road away from my burgeoning family. Of the fifty-two weeks in a year, I was on the road, often on the other side of the world, for thirty-two or thirty-three of those weeks. Now, it is a challenge to be an involved parent from that kind of distance, as I'm sure you'd agree.

But I was committed.

This all happened when my oldest son was about six or seven. We spoke daily, at least twice. He gave me updates on his life, and I shared (responsibly) about mine. One of the first things I did was remove the language about "missing" him. When I looked at that in the cold light of day, I realized we were using our moments together to lament the moments we were not together. It seemed such a waste of our very precious time. Instead, I focused on enjoying whatever time I did have with him, laughing, telling him of my love for him and what I had planned for my return, with plenty of room for him to communicate anything that was on his mind or bothering him.

Now you have to remember, I was knee-deep in my own personal transformation, with my self-awareness starting to go through the roof. This was really the first time in my life when my concern for others far outweighed any personal ones.

On one particular occasion I was in Hong Kong, in my hotel room, twenty gazillion floors above the flurry of life far below. I opened my laptop and pressed the Skype icon with excitement at the prospect of the next twenty or thirty minutes with the little man.

Now, he was usually the first face I saw whenever I Skyped, so I was a little surprised to see his mom first when the connection went through.

"What's up?" I asked.

"We have a problem," she replied.

My heart sank, I'm freaking thousands of miles away in the South China Sea, so if there's some kind of problem here, what can I realistically do? Powerless again, I guess.

"Little man gave his teacher some lip here today at school."

This was totally out of character for him. I mean, he's the fucking golden child, right?!

My thoughts raced about what to do, so I went with my first instinct.

"Let me see him."

His cherubic wee face appeared on the screen, eyes wide and waiting for the apparently bad news.

I asked him what had happened. He explained the entire thing, and yep, no doubt about it, he was being jerky with his teacher. I swooped in clinically with his consequences.

"No PlayStation for a week."

"Okay," he flatly replied.

Immediately I'm thinking *Okay?!!! That's IT?!!!*

He seemed comfortable! Like this just wasn't bothering him in the slightest. I mean what kind of sociopath am I raising here?

"In fact, you know what, after this call you can go straight to bed too."

That velvety soft reply fell out of his mouth once again. "Okay."

WHAAATTT?!!!

I'm thinking, *Oh yeah . . . oh freaking yeah?!*

I was just about to double down with some dire ramifications when I suddenly caught myself. What am I doing here?

And then it hit me like a freight train.

I was trying to get him to cry. I had to see the hurt because in the logic I had put together over my lifetime, pain equals lesson learned. Ugh. What the fuck have I become?

I stopped myself.

A few seconds seemed like forever in the silence as I looked at him from thousands of miles and the thickness of a laptop screen separating us. I gathered my thoughts and *that* word raced across my mind in the space between one blink of an eye and the next.

Authenticity. Be authentic. This was my shot.

I took a breath and with it, my opportunity.

"Y'know how you're still working out how to be a kid?" I asked.

"Yes," he said quietly.

I told him the truth. "Well, I'm still working out how to be a dad and I don't have it all figured out yet."

"I know," he said (little fucker).

Then I asked him probably the greatest question I had ever posed to anyone.

"What do you think we should do here?"

Quick as a flash he said, "I think I should write my teacher a letter and tell her I'm sorry and then go to bed for an early night."

Holy crap. The wisdom, the connections to reality and personal integrity knocked me over.

And that's exactly what he did the next day. And while it was one small detail in his life, that conversation reached deep into my brain and changed my parenting forever. It also profoundly changed me as a man.

I immediately gave up the idea that I'm supposed to have all the answers, all the ideas, all of the solutions and common sense because the reality then (and now) is that I'm making this fucking life shit up as I go along.

What a relief! No more pretense. The weight was lifted instantly.

I could finally tell the truth to myself and others. Who was I pretending for anyway? Them? Me? Some ghost of Christmas past?

What a fucking illusion!

And now? Now I'm figuring things out, discovering new thoughts and processes and situations every single day and I'm transparent about that with some of the most important people in my life, my kids. I don't have all the answers but at the same time as I was left wondering when it was, I decided that I *needed* to have them.

I had lived with that constant pressure for most of my life and not just with my family. It was everywhere. And I know many other parents do too.

If I didn't have the answer, it seemed like I was weak or stupid or of no use to the people around me. It was a constant state of mild anxiety, creeping up and down, shaping me this way and that, and the real answer had been in front of me the entire time even though I couldn't see it.

Authentic. Tell the truth.

It opened the door to a plethora of new sentences, such as

"I don't know but I can find that out."

and

"I don't understand but I'm willing to learn."

and

"No."

Oh my God, the unseen power of "no" was a game changer too!

Particularly when I could let myself just hang out in the silence of a conversation after declining anything. I had a lifetime of explaining why, justifying myself, sometimes flat out lying to make sure people didn't think badly of me. And while I know that some of you profess to an undying don't-give-a-fuckness of what other people think, try on the idea that that's exactly what you want them to think.

Therefore you do give a fuck after all.

Freedom from Self

In my case, I no longer had to pretend or hide behind bravado or a misplaced sense of fake confidence, I could just be open and free and let people think whatever they choose to think. I didn't have to prove myself to anyone or impersonate the human being I am not. I could be me. And they could be themselves. And the entryway to that life is always truth.

I should add this little piece that comes in handy from time to time with my kids. Whenever I acknowledge my lack of this thing or that, I also lay out the land in no uncertain terms. I may not have all the answers, but we *will* be going with my answers or Mom's answers until such times as they can take the reins themselves.

Does that mean I will make mistakes? Yes. And I'm truthful about that too. I won't get everything right, but like all human beings, I'm not supposed to, I'm supposed to lead the way and deal with life as it comes. And whether they like that or not, it's how it is, and powerfully dealing with what is so is a major strength for any human being.

This brings me to what you're supposed to be doing here.

As I specified before, you cannot give your children anything. You can only demonstrate in real time what it looks like to be the kind of human being who is unencumbered by their past. You are a living testimony of what a transformed human being is, particularly with those *other* people in your life whom you may have struggled to connect with or forgive or whatever.

You basically have to be the embodiment of all that you are passing on to the next generation.

My father used to say "talk is cheap," but that's basically because we treat talk that way.

Life is simple when you are authentic. There's nothing to hide, nothing to pretend. It's not without difficulty but it will be without complexity. But what to do with your children? Love them. Forgive them. Show them what integrity is.

You can add yourself to that list too, particularly the forgiveness part. You are a human being too. You didn't get it all right before and you're likely to screw a few things up in the future too. Own it, be honest and up front, you've nothing to hide, you're a human being, not a fucking Roomba.

At home, set out the rules. Keep them few and powerful and clear and deal with them without prejudice.

I find parents by and large are much more likely to bend the rules when it is inconvenient for *them* to insist upon them. In my home the rules are the rules, they just *are*, and there is no negotiating. They're not complicated, there are not many of them, but they are just not negotiable.

Consequences are definitely on the table, though, and we treat them with a maturity and logic that respects the intelligence and commitments of everyone involved.

The Job You Didn't Plan For

There's so much to being a parent you just cannot plan for. There's the unseen and unexpected, there are the things you knew would be tough but not *that* tough. There are the tragedies and dramas and the stuff of your own that came vomiting in the most unpredictable and unforeseen ways and through all of it you're supposed to get the job done.

What's the job? That they come out of this robust and equipped and while they, like all people, will have their scars and bumps (as they're supposed to), they are grounded in who they authentically are and why they are because they witnessed you handle it too, all of which brings me full circle to the single most important part of this phenomenon.

As they experience the wave coming ashore and into their world, they will experience real change, a shift in who they are for themselves, who *you* are to them, and an impending desire to move on.

As we've already seen and as I'm sure you can imagine, there is a lot of impact on not only the kid but also everyone else around them, you included.

Many times that requires the young person to make their parents wrong for all they did or did not do. Some of it you might think is completely without merit, some you may agree with, but in either case, you cannot make *them* wrong. Arguing your case is, frankly, just a fucking stupid thing to do.

Make space. Get them. Get their world, what they're dealing with, and shut the hell up. Does that mean they will make mistakes? Highly likely. But at least you'll be around to help them piece things together rather than being one more problem for them to deal with.

If their remit is to explore the ever-increasing divide between their family and their own future, it's your job to first ensure you are not widening that gap and secondly to take care of the most important part of this equation.

The road back.

Whether you agree or not, or like it or not, your children are not yours. They're not a possession or a measure of how good a person you are or something to bump up your standing in the community. Most people would deny such a notion, but if you scratch at your own view for a minute or two, you'll see yourself in this. We are all going around in life playing to an imaginary audience anyway. And while you may experience pride and satisfaction for one thing or another, what works is to see all of that as *their* accomplishments, not yours.

What about your sacrifices? What about your work and attention and commitments? You don't get to be a parent without them, and not everyone will thank you for them or at times even notice anything you did. It's a parent thing. Ask yours; they'll tell you.

This might be a good time for you to communicate your gratitude to your parents. They made their mistakes, you've made yours; who is to blame is irrelevant, those days are over. This is now on you to complete the circle. To make sure they know they got their job done with you. You see, this is not just about completing your past. This is about generosity and having a heart bigger than anything life can throw at you and being a full-blown expression of a new future instead of the lamentable Band-Aided version you have pursued until now.

To be the kind of human being you would want your kid to be whenever they get emotionally stuck.

Freedom is in the doing, not the feeling.

Your children? You love them with all you got and you let them go without condition and if their departure is marred by upset or scandal or disagreement you make sure the road back to you is an easy one for them to take. That they do not have to overcome resentment or swallow pride or ask for anything from anyone.

That the line from them to you is clean, unbroken, and available to them at any time of their choosing.

And when they do choose, you'll know they have the single most important attribute any human being can have.

The ability to change their mind, and with it, their life. They in turn will give you the biggest gift you can ever give anyone. The gift of knowing yourself as a source of unconditional, relentless love, regardless of what happened.

Job done.

"What we call the beginning is often the end. And to make an end is to make a beginning. The end is where we start from."

—T. S. Eliot

ABOUT THE AUTHOR

Born and raised in Glasgow, Scotland, Gary moved to the United States in 1997. This opened up his pathway to the world of personal development, specifically to his love of ontology and phenomenology. This approach, in which he rigorously trained for a number of years, saw him rise to become a senior program director with one of the world's leading personal development companies. After years of facilitating programs for thousands of people all over the world and later studying and being influenced by the philosophies of Martin Heidegger, Hans-Georg Gadamer, and Edmund Husserl, Gary is producing his own brand of "urban philosophy." His lifelong commitment to shifting people's ability to exert real change in their lives drives him each and every day. He has a no-frills, no-bullshit approach that has brought him an ever-increasing following drawn to the simplicity and real-world use of his work.

Survival Manuals for Everyone:

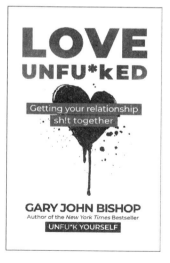

Available wherever books, ebooks, and audiobooks are sold.